# NEUTRAL ACCENT

Duke University Press   Durham and London   2015

# NEUTRAL

## ACCENT

*How Language, Labor, and Life Become Global*

A. Aneesh

© 2015 Duke University Press
All rights reserved
Printed in the United States of America on acid-free paper ∞

Typeset in Myriad Pro and Quadraat by Graphic Composition, Inc.
Library of Congress Cataloging-in-Publication Data
Aneesh, A. (Aneesh), 1964–
Neutral accent : how language, labor, and life become global / A. Aneesh.
pages cm
Includes bibliographical references and index.
ISBN 978-0-8223-5846-6 (hardcover : alk. paper)
ISBN 978-0-8223-5853-4 (pbk. : alk. paper)
ISBN 978-0-8223-7571-5 (e-book)
1. Call center agents—India—Gurgaon. 2. Call centers—India—Gurgaon.
3. Globalization. 4. Intercultural communication. i. Title.
HE8789.14A54 2015
381′.1—dc23
2014046257

Cover art: BPO, Bangalore, Kamataka, India. Photo by IndiaPicture/UIG via Getty Images.

FOR ELIJAH, until the last breath and after

# CONTENTS

## ACKNOWLEDGMENTS

Had I not taken half a dozen years to complete this book, I would have prevented names from slipping through the cracks in memory, and I will not have to face the anxiety of ingratitude. Perhaps I needed to start an acknowledgment section before starting the manuscript, as debts began to accumulate long before the manuscript took shape. Now I succumb to the cheap trick of apologizing to those whose help, though scattered through the pages ahead, remains unacknowledged.

Let me begin by thanking the MacArthur Foundation for funding field research in India, including research assistance, equipment, and all other expenses during 2004–5 (Grant No. 03–80081–000–GSS). I also thank two research assistants, Sabil Francis and Rosmin Matthew, who were graduate students at Jawaharlal Nehru University at the time, and partners in research.

A couple of years later I was fortunate to receive a resident fellowship at the School for Advanced Research (SAR) in Santa Fe, allowing me to reflect back on field research, analyze the material, read a lot, and write a bit. I felt deeply supported by the SAR's president at the time, James Brooks, and his sociologist wife, Rebecca Allahyari, who made critical comments and suggestions on early presentations and writing. I must also thank my colleagues at the SAR— Graham St. John, Barbara Rose Johnston, Eric Haanstad, Noenoe K. Silva, Julie Velasquez—whose intellectual and gastronomical companionship was crucial to that magical year of contemplation and New Mexican cuisine. Had I concentrated less on eating out in Santa Fe, I would have probably completed the manuscript in 2007. But I needed the good fortune, once again, to receive fellowships from the Center for 21st Century Studies (2008–9), and from the Global Studies Program at the University of Wisconsin-Milwaukee (2010–11) that helped me bring this project to completion.

Before I began field research in 2004, I was grateful to Akhil Gupta for his suggestion to do a focused ethnography of call centers. This book owes its realization to that casual conversation over lunch at Stanford where I taught at the time. I have also benefited from presenting various aspects of this research at many conferences, including American Sociological Association, American Anthropological Association, Association for Asian Studies, Society for the Social Study of Science as well as many university campuses where I was invited for lectures and presentations.

This book includes in bits and pieces some of my earlier ideas and writings published in journals. I thank the editors and publishers for an early appreciation of those ideas. Particularly, I express gratitude to the editors and publishers of *Frakcija* (2007) and the *Journal of Social Issues* (2012) for publishing my articles on global communication, *Sociological Theory* (2009) for an article on the concept of algocracy. I also thank my coeditors, Patrice Petro and Lane Hall, and the publisher of a volume titled *Beyond Globalization: Making New Worlds in Media* (2011) for allowing me to introduce globalization as multiple worlds of differentiated reality.

I thank the anonymous reviewers of the manuscript for their incredibly crucial feedback on early as well as final drafts. And let me not forget Duke editor, Courtney Berger, for her constant support of this project throughout these years, and Erin Hanas for her help during manuscript preparation and production. The manuscript would not be the same without Gillian Hillis's meticulous copyediting.

I am grateful to call center agents, some of whom became friends during the year of field research. I also appreciate the always supportive department of sociology at the University of Wisconsin-Milwaukee, particularly Deborah Ritchie Kolberg and Alexander Taylor for their help with various aspects of this manuscript. I would also like to thank my brother-in-law, J. R. Mohan, for putting me in touch with some call center executives. My final thanks go to Erica Bornstein, who has continued through the jagged journey of life to be my guiding North Star.

Most accounts of globalization are accounts of connections, integrations, and flows. Since the advent of the web the world has appeared as a unity, networked and engaged. India's call centers in particular have come to represent a remarkable global shift: for the first time in history, mundane customer interactions have begun to happen across continents in real time. From global commerce to social media, the idea of society is increasingly bypassing the boundaries of nations, cities, or local communities. Many alternative accounts of this society have emerged: information society, risk society, network society, cosmopolitan society, and world society.

Yet the emergent reality of unprecedented economic, political, technological, and cultural interconnections cannot be understood, in my view, without paying equal attention to global differentiations and separations. Economic or cultural integrations often come at a cost whose accounting is one of the purposes behind writing this book. Just as air travel—while connecting us to distant lands—also disconnects our circadian clocks from day-night cycles, leaving us jet lagged, there are durable disconnections produced by certain global connections. India's call centers in their distinctive complexity allow me to explore such disconnections on several registers— place, language, labor, identity, and the body.

Call centers are a small part of India's business process outsourcing (BPO) industry, an industry that generated $14.1 billion of export revenue and accounted for 34 percent of the worldwide BPO market in 2010, employing, directly or indirectly, over 4.5 million people (Nasscom 2011). The BPO industry owes its rise to the economic liberalization program started in 1991 by the Indian government on the verge of default on external payment liabilities, gradually opening the economy to global markets. Inspired by a number of government schemes, for example, tax holidays, export processing, and special economic zones (Aneesh 2006; Palit and Bhattacharjee 2008), the BPO industry has garnered worldwide attention with its ability to bypass traditional barriers to labor market globalization. It is not surprising that these call centers have come under scrutiny in public debates about outsourcing (Bhagwati, Panagariya, and Srinivasan 2004), and a growing body of scholarship has begun to review their complex terrain (Basi 2009; Das, Dharwadkar, and Brandes 2008; Krishnamurthy 2004; Mirchandani 2012; Mukherjee 2008; Patel 2010; Poster and Wilson 2008; Taylor and Bain 2005; Upadhya and Vasavi 2008).

Being some of the few sites where different languages, accents, cultures, laws, and economies interact on a daily basis, call centers are particularly interesting places to study how the place-bound complex of speech, identity, and the laboring body yields to processes of global integration. I conducted a yearlong ethnography of call centers in Gurgaon, India. Ethnography tends to be a good fit for inquiries about social processes. Such inquiries highlight the importance of understanding "something" in which the process manifests itself, and these "somethings"—for example, the emergence of national societies—may be called social formations (Glaeser 2005). To focus on the interaction rituals of an emerging global social formation, this research included fifty in-depth formal interviews with agents as well as managers from five call centers. But the most important aspect of field research was participant observation through personal employment at a call center for several months.

### A Neutral Accent

In the winter of 2005, while investigating India's call centers in New Delhi, my research assistant, a sharp and unreserved Indian graduate student, made a suggestion: "Why don't you try to get a job at a call center? You don't look your age, and you speak with a slight American accent. Any company would give you the job." I followed the suggestion. I had conducted quite a few interviews with workers and executives by this time and thought I had fair knowledge of this nocturnal world, but I had no feel for the floor, for the immediate experience of connecting live with customers across the globe.

I started by applying for the position of voice and accent trainer at a major call center, Datys, in Gurgaon, a city bursting at the seams with economic exuberance. While my credentials—having lived in the United States for over a decade—were impressive, I was not offered the position even after three interviews. A snippet from the third interview may explain why:

"Could you stop using that American accent?" my interviewer, Payal, a senior trainer in her thirties, asked me.

"What do you mean?" I said.

"I mean, can you stop rolling your R's as Americans do, and start using a neutral accent, instead," she said brusquely.

"But there is no such thing as a neutral accent." I failed to control my intellectual righteousness, even though this was not the occasion for academic debate.

"Well, there is. Do you hear how I'm speaking? Plain and neutral English," Payal said.

"You mean plain, Indian English," I said.

"Yes, Indian English is global English. It is neither American nor British," she proudly claimed.

The interview continued on its downhill course for another hour without either of us ceding our respective positions. Sacrificing my job prospect at the altar of my academic convictions, I tried to convince her that all speech was accented, and the native speakers of American English would clearly detect an accent in her English, but she continued to claim that she spoke "global English," an English from nowhere, perfected through the neutralization of her regional accent.

A few days after the interview, however, my intellectual scorn gave way to a grudging admiration. While it might be easy for a sociolinguist to dispute her claims, Payal did bring to light an important aspect of call centers: the creation of a neutralized space for communication across cultures. Neutrality, I would soon discover, was not only the crux of understanding call centers; it was also key to comprehending globalization itself. It was crucial to understanding the unhinging of accents from places, identities from persons, and persons from their biological clocks. These unhingings relating to speech, identity, place, and the body underpin much of what this book is about. Globalization, in this view, is a force of history urging us not toward homogenization but toward new differentiations—a form of language, for instance, constructed as neutral—functioning on a global scale.

I needed to rethink my insistence that there was no neutral accent. Generally, accents have developed because speech tended to be place-bound, acquiring a peculiar flavor through countless repetitions in face-to-face interactions within a small radius of habitation. But, in itself, an accent is not an accent at all. An accent becomes an accent only when transportation allows one to cross regions of speech; it is an accent only when juxtaposed with others. No wonder accents carry information about their place of origin, allowing us to say, "I can tell where you are from!" With the construction of a neutral accent, we can imagine the development of placeless accents—placeless, not in the sense that it is from no place, but rather that hearers cannot place it. If call centers in India attempt to scrub off the marks of an accent's place of origin and establish the resulting pronunciation as neutral, that accent does, for the future, become neutral for its own purposes. Such an accent does not allude to a preexisting reality; it produces it. Reality begins to conform to this performance; not completely, not without failures, but people start acting in ways that push the accent toward the ideal of neutrality.

After an hour Payal gave up on me, asking me to complete a voice and accent training module before she could further consider my candidacy. It was an odd request, since it required substantial work without the promise of any reward. Soon I gave up on landing the trainer job and instead focused on obtaining a position as an ordinary agent. Initially, my research assistant and I went to four or five recruitment sessions, two of which were organized by specific recruitment agencies where we observed the interview process as well as interactions among prospective candidates. At J-Tech's office, sessions ran at full capacity. I counted about fifty applicants, some sitting but most standing, in a very small office space. Most of the applicants were men. All were young and brimming with cautious energy. This was a scene for walk-in interviews. The wait was long. After a while we found it awkward to stand and decided just to sit on the carpeted floor. The receptionist told me it would take at least one hour before we could expect our turn. Despite the rapid expansion of the BPO industry by 2005, there was a steady stream of applicants for the jobs that they offered. It seemed the supply for call center jobs still exceeded the demand. Applicants were supposed to come with a resume and a passport size photograph in hand. While waiting with others, I struck up conversations with two male applicants. Both were applying for web-based processes. When I asked them what the recruitment agency charged them as a placement fee, they replied that the agency charged the companies for whom it was recruiting.

After a couple of such visits to recruitment offices, I found myself working for GoCom, a middle-of-the-road company in size and revenue, that employed about one thousand agents when I was there in 2005. Located in Udyog Vihar in Gurgaon, where many software and service firms are based, GoCom provided services for clients based in the United Kingdom and United States and specialized in telemarketing services, mostly pertaining to mobile phone connections but also to reselling mortgages. I worked at GoCom for several months, starting as a voice, accent, and process trainee and eventually moving to the floor to make telemarketing calls.

During training I was part of a cohort of eight men and five women, all young, spirited, and fresh out of college (except for me, of course). Working as an ordinary agent, I attended lectures and hands-on sessions with other trainees pertaining to voice and accent as well as process training. I participated in mock calls, later "barging in" on live calls made on the floor by trained agents. Being part of the telemarketing campaign, these calls were initiated at our end (employee-initiated or by a dialing program), carrying an incentive for a successful sale. While my personal experience was limited to such outbound calls, I interviewed many agents who were in charge of inbound calls and engaged in casual conversation with them as they practiced their accents and memorized different elements of new processes and culture.

The training period was full of cheer and angst. This was the time when the group developed solidarity against their common opponent, the trainer, and took longer than permitted breaks between sessions. These breaks included tea, coffee, smoking, and even singing. This is where I met some of the people—Vikas, Tarun, Narayan, Mukul, and others—whose work lives color many of these pages. I followed them to their shared apartments in Gurgaon and sat around "soaking and poking," to use Richard Fenno's phrase (1978, 247), while they talked about their experiences. I ate with them in the cafeteria where lunch was served after midnight. At GoCom as well as at other call centers, men appeared to outnumber women substantially, though women's participation was reported to be growing quickly. In countless conversations, agents revealed their commitment to, and perceptions of this career, and about their own backgrounds and goals in life. I also collected materials such as training manuals and class notes from my own participation as well as from two other call center agents.

This was a highly social and lively group, quite typical of India's college graduates. Yet, as I witnessed, the trainees sometimes found it difficult to suppress the effects of their first language—Hindi, Bangla or Punjabi—on their second language, English, and to overcome their style of speech, which bore clear marks of their upbringing. English is no ordinary second language on the continent, as every Indian would testify; it is also a measure of success and status, an accepted border between classes, a statement of both personal and parental accomplishments. Among a large body of India's non-English speakers, it remains very much an imperial language. Growing up in India, I remember my distress at being spoken to in English. Having attended "Hindi-medium schools" for my entire education until college, I could never respond in English. In panic, I would forget even the simple sentences I had learnt while taking English in school. These occasional non-conversations in English would put me crushingly in my place. English was a probing measure of personal worth. Later, preparing for a history exam in the eighties, I wondered at the forethought of Lord Macaulay who in his famous Minute on Indian Education delivered in 1835 encouraged the British "to do our best to form a class who may be interpreters between us and the millions whom we govern; a class of persons, Indian in blood and colour, but English in taste, in opinions, in morals, and in intellect." English has since attained a dual status: it has made the non-English speaking majority—over 80 percent of the population—feel smaller and inferior in their lack of English knowledge. "It is a peculiar sensation," Du Bois described the condition well, "this double-consciousness, this sense of always looking at one's self through the eyes of others, of measuring one's soul by the tape of a world that looks on in amused contempt and pity" (Du Bois 2003).

On the other hand, the development of English in India has also proved Macaulay wrong. To a degree, English has also become, despite its imperial burden, a language of possibility in India, a promise of modernity, a move away from old and oppressive spaces of social life, injustices of gender, humiliations of caste, and bigotry of various kinds. This class of English speakers does not only offer arbiters of the ruling elite; it also provides activists and scholars who have challenged old and new power hierarchies. To a non-speaker, however, the ability of English to bully them into psychological submission is quite remarkable.

Some of my coworkers at GoCom spoke English only haltingly, not because they had not attended English-medium schools, but because they had attended the ordinary ones or were not keen students, or both. But even the ones who were fluent in English lacked the cultural grammar of places they were about to serve. Despite the trainer's warning, the trainees kept using "sir" in every sentence to address the mock customer. The use of "sir" in India has connotations of accepted hierarchy that appear off-key in the context of American notions of social equality. This aspect of communication leads to a larger question of how cultures—separated by distance, norms, and values—could talk. In the absence of a common national, ethnic, or organizational culture across continents, what makes communication possible among social worlds technologically integrated in real time?

## Global Communication

The problem of communication is a tough one even within a shared cultural framework: before I speak I must anticipate what you anticipate about my possible expression, making communication a highly improbable event. For example, a man addressing a woman (or vice versa) at a bar must carefully anticipate how his definition of the situation will be realized on the other side; that is, he must do something impossible: read her mind before every act of speech. Usually, cultural norms rush to help, keeping an appearance of order. But lacking common norms across vastly different societies, what makes communication possible among persons technologically hitched in real time?

In popular scholarly accounts (McLuhan 1994; Negroponte 1995), it is often assumed that once data-communication links have been established, global integration—the global village—will of necessity follow. This assumption ignores the work that goes into social and cultural integration. For example, when an agent in Gurgaon, India, donning a headset connected to a computer, seeks to sell a mobile phone connection to an American in Indianapolis, how can they converse with each other? How can they anticipate each other's attitude upon which their own response is contingent? While technologies of communication have created new opportunities for routine human interaction on a global scale, technologies per se do not guarantee effective communication.

What facilitated their conversation—a riddle I attempt to solve in chapter 3—was a set of inventions in global communication, allowing the conversation to jump over the hurdles of ordinary language and speech. After witnessing training sessions at GoCom, I realized that transnational business practices relied on the transmutation of cultural communication into global communication through the processes of neutralization and mimesis. Neutralization refers to attempts at paring down unwanted cultural particulars (e.g., accents) while mimesis refers to attempts at mimicking desired cultural elements (e.g., politeness). Agents at GoCom, and indeed, every call center in India, worked hard to scrub off itineraries of their childhood socialization, culture, and styles of speech. Their training in global communication was thus not a simple matter of learning new organizational rules, regulations, or work processes. It also required the adoption of a foreign cultural logic, bordering on new identity and personhood.

## Differentiating Identity

The Indian calling agents I observed and worked with were required to change accents, acquire pseudonyms, work hard to know a place they would never visit, learn work skills not portable to any other industry, and labor at night when the world outside their building was asleep. But we must not think of call center agents as blue-collar factory workers. The workplace culture and identity of these workers, as Carla Freeman (2000) in her account of transnational work has pointed out, was closer to white-collar professional workers. Yet contortions of identity shift were instructive. Their cultural competence in their existing milieu was an impediment in the new work situation. Little by little, they learned the ways of their new world. Practicing accents, memorizing informal phrases, learning different styles of speech and geographies of the places abroad, including street designations and state capitals, these agents moved between their social identity in Gurgaon and an identity conducive to global communication.

But what was equally remarkable was the customer side of global integration. The question of identity was not limited to Indian calling agents; it also affected their American customers in a very different manner, as I explain in chapter 4, for they were transformed into their system profiles. Indeed, a call center agent was not the one who dialed their number. It was a software program called the "Dialer," which targeted specific American profiles, according to credit history, age, gender, region, education, and buying patterns. Most telemarketing calls, originating from India or the United States, aimed at mirrors of identity in which actual persons suddenly found themselves involved. This global conversation seemed to happen between system identities—identities developed for global systems—in which persons found themselves implicated.

Global communication, in this context, seems both a failure and a success. It fails daily when cultural differences between Indian agents and their American customers get the better of its neutralizing mechanisms. Many American companies do not renew contracts with their Indian service providers if their workforce fails to provide quality service in a functioning accent. Yet it has effectively created a system of communication, reflected in the Indian industry's phenomenal 30 percent annual growth in its first decade, whose disturbing ripples are felt on American shores.

## The Problem of Successful Integration

India's call centers exploded on American consciousness during the presidential election of 2004 amid heated debates on job outsourcing. Sure enough, by 2008 most Americans have had personal experiences—good or bad—with calls to or from an Indian call center; everyone has an anecdote to recount. When I was interviewed on a public radio talk show in the summer of 2006, I was taken aback by the flood of callers who had something to say, not neutral to be sure, about India's call centers. Yet few callers realized that the matter was far more important than the quality of service or diversion of their calls to another country. The reason they were talking with someone across the globe was not a simple cost-saving corporate decision. The interaction was enabled by a far more fundamental transformation that allows parts of identity to be differentiated out of one's personhood—records of my financial, medical, traveling, and residential history facing me as an alien entity in corporate or state possession, and targeted for a phone call by various interests. Thus, the innovation did not simply lie in diverting calls from the United States to India. The primary innovation lay in turning identities into programmable events for use within the framework of databases differentiated for the purposes of finance, medicine, law, and consumption. Just as parts of personhood were detached from their social location for the purpose of global integration, one could also see how the diurnal body was unmoored from its temporal location through night work in call centers.

Let us pay attention for a moment to the laboring body and how it becomes global. As India's call centers are connected live with divergent timetables of London, New York, Seattle, or Sydney, their agents must work at different hours of the night to serve their overseas customers. This global integration of different time zones requires the diurnal body to perform nocturnal labor, disconnecting and placing it into conflict with its own sur-roundings. With the growing neutrality toward the diurnal character of the body, working at odd hours or at night has become common in global and nonglobal contexts. While the regime of night work can be traced to the commercialization of the electric light bulb in the nineteenth century, its growth and expansion in the last few decades has been phenomenal. Harriet Presser (2003) in *Working in a 24/7 Economy* notes that two-fifths of Ameri-cans work mostly during evenings, nights, or weekends, or on rotating shifts outside the traditional work day.

Indeed, night work has become so entrenched in the global economy that there is no single vantage point left to make a blanket criticism. We cannot unequivocally criticize night work as problematic just because it conflicts with the body's circadian rhythms. We may have had a century of struggle for an eight-hour day, but we may not see, as I contend in chapter 5, any resistance to what Murray Melbin (1987) called the colonization of the night. Arguments and criticisms themselves develop conflicting crite-ria of justification with no consensus on the topic of human well-being, which seems to split off in three different directions: social well-being, economic well-being, and physical well-being. While night work allows an individual to hold a job with clear economic well-being, it also indicates a simultaneous isolation from larger daytime social life, an unhinging of family life when it is difficult for spouses to be together and for parents to be home with their children, reducing their social well-being. For a natural scientist, too, night work reduces well-being but in a physical way, as it is in conflict with the body's natural circadian rhythms and its irrefutable diurnal frame, which is organized around light-dark cycles. While night work increases economic well-being, it reduces social and physical well-being.

India's call centers are clearly an ideal location to witness global transfor-mations as reflected in separations of cultural and neutral accents, of social, bureaucratic, and system identities, of diurnal body and nocturnal work, and of economic, social, and physical knowledge production. Instead of empha-sizing socio-technical hybridity, I hope to highlight the separation of differ-ent realms that call centers appear to display more clearly. Such separations are taken up in different chapters, each shedding light on divergent tracks and independent itineraries. The concept of neutrality binds the entire proj-ect together by showing how the realms are not merely differentiating but also increasingly neutral to each other. The systemic neutrality among globally differentiating realms constitutes the theoretical arc of the book. I analyze neutrality both as an abstract notion and an experienced dissonance. In the epilogue, I attempt a theoretical analysis of neutrality by construing it as indifference to difference, zooming out of the specific landscape of call centers to place these developments in a global context.

At its core, then, this book is not about call centers, or not simply about them. For a focused understanding of call centers, there have emerged wonderful texts in the last couple of years. Shezhad Nadeem (2011) has explored the implications of cultural mimicry in making "dead ringers" out of Indian call center agents. Kiran Mirchandani (2012) has highlighted the dynamics of race, nation, and identity in a shifting managerial strategy toward subtle and covert practice of enacting Americanness through recruitment and training, demeanor and scripting, office ambiance and architectural decor. Earlier, Winifred Poster (2007) captured the globalization of service work through what she called "national identity management." Two monographs by Tina Basi (2009) and Reena Patel (2010) underscore the impact of call center industry on women's lives outside of work as they navigate urban spaces. These and other texts, including my previous articles (Aneesh 2007, 2012), are much more attentive to the study of call center employment. This book, however, is not a study of call centers in their own right but a study that sheds light on differentiations that provide the axes for global integration.

Why study call centers, then, one may ask? India's call centers, in my view, combine many aspects—real-time connection, cultural heterogeneity, global commerce in databases—that in their unique complexity hold important clues to our present, and likely foreshadow the future. They demonstrate a peculiar paradox: dysfunctions of a world gone zealously functional, a paradox easier to spot and study in India's call centers, a paradox that plays out in the lives of call center agents and increasingly, I argue, in all our lives.

This book, thus, tells a story not of failures of global integration, or the abiding persistence of digital divide. Rather, it narrates the problem of successful integration, the global economy's functional triumphs, and durable disconnections produced by connections. At the level of personal relationships, Sherry Turkle (2012) has already offered a sobering account of human disconnectedness in the middle of virtual connections. I attempt to change the scale and type of disconnection as I explore varied realms of the city, identity, language, and the body. The next chapter begins with the city of Gurgaon, the largest hub of India's call centers, and its urban differentiations bearing marks of the global age. Operating in American, British, or Australian time zones, Gurgaon's call centers are unique, previously unavailable, sites for examining the point of global contact where cultures are forced to make sense of each other through mechanisms provided by the culture of capitalism. The city is a suitable candidate for beginning this inquiry as it illuminates the still hazy interstices from which the present age is gradually emerging.

## Glimpsing an Urban Future: *Divergent Tracks of Gurgaon*

As late as the 1980s Gurgaon was a sunstruck expanse of fertile earth at the empty edges of New Delhi. A small town with a smaller bazaar crowded with tea shops selling samosas and jalebis, small clothing stores, tailors, paan stalls, and old-style jewelers—a place full of bustle but, oddly, in no particular hurry. It was a noisy place, by western standards, but a whisper away from the bazaar lay quiet fields of green in seasonal incarnations of wheat, paddy, and pulses. Being next to a major metropolis, Gurgaon struggled to define itself, often leaning toward the character of Haryana, the agrarian state of sun-hardened folks whose straight talk aroused suspicions of rudeness, and whose culture was labeled "agri-culture" by the cultured populace of Delhi. Before Biharis started arriving in large numbers, migrants from Haryana were the people considered responsible for destroying Delhi's possible urbanity and refinement. Gurgaon, on the other hand, remained untouched by Delhi. Indeed, if a place worth any mention must have a past that connects to a seat of empire, religion, or trade, Gurgaon—a place of ordinary hard-working peasantry—was a nonplace on the cultural map of India. Just a couple of decades ago!

FIGURE I.I. Old Gurgaon

Gurgaon is still a nonplace but for reasons of a different kind. The problem is no longer about the past of no particular consequence, no major monuments of the Sultanate or Mughal times, or pilgrimages leading to Gurgaon, reconstructing the past through a collective renewal of memory. The city has, in fact, outgrown the need of a past for self-definition. It is defined by its future. As the future can never fully exist in the present but can only be imagined or glimpsed as a not-yet present, Gurgaon gains its full meaning only as a virtual city, as a place that exceeds its appearances.

It is not surprising that Gurgaon is a city of glass, crowded with buildings reflecting more than they contain, referring not to the past but to prospects briefly glimpsed in their flashy façade. Borrowed from colder climates of the West, its glassy architecture alone does not mark Gurgaon as a nonplace.

It gains the character of a nonplace through its evasion of memory and roots. Despite good agriculture, its life is no longer rooted in its fertile soil or its local bazaars; it is a global city of an export variety whose capacity for capital generation is increasingly dependent on the flows from across the seas. Its economy is intertwined with other economies in real time, and hence susceptible to global vicissitudes. It has become global

FIGURE I.2.
City of glass

before it could become a regional city. Gurgaon no longer looks up to Delhi for inspiration.

Many of Gurgaon's townships are named not after Delhi's plush localities; they have names that signify that the city has arrived on the global map: "Beverly Park," "Malibu Town," or "Sun City." Since the late 1990s, the city itself has been called the Millennium City, situating itself not in the history soiled by farmlands but on the horizon of a new millennium.

Gurgaon takes the logic of a modern city so far that it stops bearing resemblance to it. Let us first recognize how it remains well within Max Weber's definition of a city, medieval or modern, that is, primarily a market settlement where "the local population satisfies an economically significant part of its everyday requirements in the local market," and where "a significant part of the products bought there were acquired or produced specifi-

FIGURE 1.3. Beverly Park II

cally for sale on the market by local population or that of the immediate hinterland" (Weber 1921, 1213). What makes the city modern in Weber's sense is the fact that authority rests on a rational rather than on a traditional basis; the law is enforced on a universalistic basis rather than on a personal basis; and major divisions are based on class rather than family and clan. Gurgaon also remains faithful to Georg Simmel's diagnosis of the metropolis where life is coordinated less by interpersonal relationships always blemished by "irrational, instinctive, sovereign human traits"; rather, its meaning and style, its color and content, its blasé attitude, owe more to the functional mechanisms of the money economy and rationalities of "punctuality, calculability and exactness" (Simmel 1903).

Beyond these understandings, however, Gurgaon takes functional mechanisms to a new level where it appears to lose the unity of a city. It starts to reveal diverse itineraries of multiple functional worlds that give it a look of *cities within a city*, some local, others global. If global processes mean a certain unhinging of social, economic, and political relations from their local-territorial preconditions, this unraveling does not suggest that the place has turned into a void. Just as cities located on the shores of oceans and rivers and other waterways developed a particular port-city form, we can explore Gurgaon as a city located at the nexus of global information highways, signaling a set of connections different from the ones that defined a regular city. To substantiate how global interactions reterritorialize contemporary cities and states (Brenner 2004; Harvey 1982; Sassen 1991), let me highlight Gurgaon as a variation on global cities.

I detect three essential features of Gurgaon, which may not cover all its aspects but they may help us decide if the city is part of a new urban variation that is emerging in fast-growing economies like India and China. While Gurgaon may have a lot in common with conventional cities, these three interrelated features seem to differentiate it from others. First, the shape and trim of Gurgaon is not that of a single city but a collection of mini cities. Second, the character of Gurgaon appears defined more by other places than the surrounding region. Third, the city is gradually emerging as a set of transnational enclaves, or more formally, of special economic zones (SEZs).

## An Archipelago of Mini Cities

Shuchi Nayak, a human resource manager at an international call center, rented an apartment in one of the posh residential complexes of Gurgaon. As I started all my interviews with informants' personal stories, I came to know that she lived there with her husband and a three-year-old daughter. She mentioned that there was even a room for an aayaa (i.e., maid) in her apartment but she did not want a live-in maid, leading to an interesting conversation about her apartment complex. Shuchi was a bit unusual for her social class in Gurgaon where upper middle class often shows a callous disregard for the city's poor. Born in Orissa, an eastern state of India, she received her MBA from Calcutta where she worked for four or five years before moving to Gurgaon. Raised by a progressive father who worked for the central government, Shuchi had worked as a human resource coordinator for a U.S. subsidiary, a software company, for seven years before joining the call center. Despite a high household salary, she was acutely aware of her humble background, and began to complain against the inequality that surrounded her building; just half a kilometer away from her building was a local slum that supplied aayaas and other servants to her gated complex, which was almost a self-contained mini city, with a private school, gymnasium, private club, tennis courts, swimming pool, and more important, its own infrastructural facilities, including back-up electric generator, and

FIGURE I.4. Plum City

water tanks. Such mini cities had begun mushrooming all around India's metropolitan cities. Another mini city built by DLF corporation boasted its own hospital, water recycling system, and—ahem—fire brigade.

Shuchi explained how the world looked so different outside her vast complex. There were better and safer walking paths built inside these mini cities than there were outside, and she regularly took walks that wove around a beautifully designed swimming pool and various gardens, one for every block in her mini city. If there was a power outage, an everyday event in Gurgaon, her tall housing complex did not show obvious signs: its lights stayed on, its Internet and air conditioners continued running, and its elevators kept quietly ascending and descending.

Such mini cities have proliferated all over in India since the 1990s. They are paragons of what an ideal and aesthetically pleasing small city—with no class divide, educated inhabitants, and functioning infrastructure—must look like but has become a futile hope in much of India. It was, however, not too difficult to see that the rise of these plum cities was intricately linked to the proliferation of its opposite: slum cities. Slums lacked everything that plum cities enjoyed: electricity, water, and basic sanitation. But they were

FIGURE I.5. Laborers

essential to Gurgaon's plum cities, for the slum dwellers had been building
the city with their cheap labor since the late 1980s, raising towers by hand,
literally, brick by brick, building it so that there would be no place left for
them to live there.

Once the township was finished, their presence in the complex changed
its character. Now their movements were watched with suspicion. They
must get their identity checked at the gate when they entered or exited the
township. The security guards at the gate, most of whom lived in slum cities,
made sure the workers left carrying nothing more than what they had entered with. In the period between entering and leaving, they cooked family
meals, bathed the family's children, entertained them at the playground,
mopped the floors, and watered immaculate gardens of the premises. In the
evening they came back to their shacks, a different world, where there was
no water to bathe their babies, and barely enough, courtesy of some public
faucet or biweekly supply through a water tanker, to cook a meal. As the
dusking sky quietly slipped into their shacks during long and persistent
daily power outages, their slum city fought the blinding spray of darkness
with the hesitant glow of kerosene lamps.

FIGURE I.6. Slum City

Class divides are nothing new in capitalism. Emile Zola's description of a factory settlement of the 1880s has a ring of familiarity: "The inmates lived there, elbow to elbow, from one end to the other; and no fact of family life remained hidden, even from the youngsters. In spite of the keen cold outside, there was a living heat in the heavy air, that hot stuffiness . . . the smell of human cattle" (Zola 1942, 13). Gurgaon's slum cities may not be too far from European factory settlements of the 1880s. Yet Gurgaon is quite different from those settlements. Unlike early modern European cities, Gurgaon stands at the ruins of modern hopes of integration. Modernist discourses of linear, universal development offered the hope that the fruits of growth would come to all, slowly but surely. And they often did: a universal grid of public education that sought to cover the rich and the poor, raising high school education in the United States from less than 14 percent in 1900 to 83 percent in 1999 (Chao 2001); a continuous electrical grid that ran through rich and poor areas alike; and water pipelines that did not skip the poor to hydrate the rich.

But the promise of modernity in many cases, as James Ferguson noticed in the case of Zambia, has turned out to be a broken promise: "A new generation of Zambians . . . has come of age in a world where the modernist certainties their parents grew up with have been turned upside down, a world where life expectancies and incomes shrink instead of grow, where children become less educated than their parents instead of more, where migrants move from urban centers to remote villages instead of vice versa" (Ferguson, 1999, 137).

True, Gurgaon was not located on the Zambian Copperbelt. To the contrary, it was experiencing explosive growth. But Gurgaon's growth still defied the presumed logic of modernization: Instead of continuous electricity, water supply, and sewage systems that carried the fruits of growth everywhere, it witnesses an archipelago of growth pockets where the hopes of universal urban services were replaced with private realizations of mini utopias, the specialized zones of living. Gurgaon had evolved into many cities within a city, an archipelago of cities. Neat packages of life, consumption, and work—gated townships, malls, and call centers—ensured a continuous supply of amenities to its special inhabitants. Decades ago Richard Sennett (1970) had warned us that any community purged or "purified" of the diverse and conflicting interests and personalities would be lifeless. As a bundle of different functional domains, the city appeared too specialized to be inclusive of all, poor and rich, leaving migrant labor from poorer parts of India out of the urban dream that Gurgaon had become. Harassed by the police as potential criminals, they were building cities not designed for them.

Priced out of Gurgaon's real estate boom where property prices in a mini city like Shuchi's doubled and tripled every five years, the poor inhabited the fringes of Gurgaon's growth islands, but they found themselves frequently at the center of its troubles, often blamed for illegally siphoning off power from the main electric lines that were supposed to skip their slum dwellings, a common middle-class complaint in many cities of India.

Large enclaves of affluence have emerged not only in Gurgaon but around all fast-growing, overstrained Indian cities like Delhi, Mumbai, and Bangalore. It is a larger urban formation where islands of affluence, secured against the encroachments of the slums, come equipped with amenities not available even to their Western counterparts: a regiment of maids and drivers supplied by slum cities.

My contention that Gurgaon represented an urban formation with an appearance of a city containing mini cities is well supported by large-scale real estate developers who regularly use city and township in their self-descriptions, distinguishing cities and townships from other kinds of developments: "Suncity Projects Pvt Ltd, is a pioneer in conceiving and executing a profusion of urbane real estate projects, arraying from *Townships* to *Group housing* to *luxury Apartments* to *shopping Malls* to *Office Complexes*" (emphasis added). They also describe the meaning of mini city better than this author:

> The Suncity Gurgaon is spread over 140 acres of lush green environs in Gurgaon, promising the best of international quality residential and commercial possessions. The magnificently planned township offers plots, built up floors, apartments, penthouses, shops, etc. offering all the best facilities that any township can boast of. It plans to provide exceptional amenities like—clubhouse, schools, hospital, shopping center and dispensary. It facilitates drip irrigation and water harvesting systems, parks and jogging trails, wide roads, 100% Power backup, for group housing & commercial, ample parking space and round-the-clock security. (Suncity 2012)

Here is another description from DLF's plan of their Gardencity in Gurgaon:

> The pioneers of plotted developments proudly bring to you a community where you can live luxuriously in the lap of greens. Enhanced by about 1000 acres of planned open spaces, a panorama that's the size of DLF Phase I and II put together, DLF Gardencity gives you a chance to capture the grandeur of nature in your neighbourhood. The buildings are grouped to form blocks that have internal courtyards. Each block would have a unique character distinguished by gardens, recreational facilities, etc. Parking for each block is provided in two levels below the interior court gardens: Gated Community; Over 3100 apartments by DLF nearing delivery in adjoining areas; 4 acres of Retail complex planned on the lines of Galleria abutting Gardencity; Adjoining 100 acres greenbelt with in the vicinity; Host of Community facilities such as School, Playground etc.; Minutes drive to airport via Dwarka Expressway; Includes park; Water bodies; Lakes; Sports ground; Stadium. (DLF 2012)

Despite the unavoidable hyperbole of advertisement, the privatized development of city-like structures has its basis in persistent failures of central and state governments in matters of infrastructure, failures known and experienced by all and sundry, differentiating India even within the BRICS (Brazil, Russia, India, China, South Africa) group.

In addition to private islands of habitation, there have also emerged many islands of consumption, developed by some of the same real estate players.

Indeed, Gurgaon is often called the mall capital of India. On the heels of an information technology-enabled BPO boom, Gurgaon has led India in an organized retail boom, which is also its largest industry after IT services.

## An Archipelago of Malls

With more than twelve million retail stores, India may be called a nation of shopkeepers, a term once derisively used by Napoleon for England ("L'Angleterre est une nation de boutiquiers"). Shops are small and many, primarily managed by independent owners. With about eleven retail shops per thousand persons, India has the highest shop density in the world; that is, one shop for every twenty to twenty-five families. Its cities boast of much higher density. Delhi, for example, has about forty-five shops per thousand persons. Americans, arguably the biggest shoppers in the world, must make do with only about four shops per thousand populations (Srivastava 2008). While India is the second-largest consumer market and seventh-largest retail market in the world (Pick and Müller 2011), employing almost 21 million people in the retail industry, only about 4 percent of retail stores are part of the organized retail—big chains and showrooms (Srivastava 2008). The majority of shops belongs to a long tradition of kirana stores (mom and pop stores), street hawkers, roadside stalls, and weekly markets. Yet, in less than a decade, from just a couple of indoor malls in 2000, the number of malls in India, according to CBRE Commercial Real Estate Services, is estimated to touch 280 in 2012 (TOI 2010). Gurgaon alone has more than 40 malls, selling Versace and Gucci in places where cattle fairs were once held.

Let us give this transformation a moment of reflection. Perhaps a personal story may help. My connection with Gurgaon is older than this research conducted in 2004–5. In 1992 after undergoing training for the Indian Civil Services, my first job posting landed me in Gurgaon. My office was located in what may now be called old Gurgaon. At the time, we watched with fascination the emergence of new residential and business sectors on the remote periphery of the town. Maruti Suzuki Company, India's biggest car maker, was already operating in Udyog Vihar (business park), but a bigger transformation was in the air as policies of liberalization took shape at the national level. My official driver, Sardar Singh, had just sold his farmland to a real estate developer of malls for two million rupees, an amount I could barely dream of as a government officer in those days. Sardar didn't quit his job, though, waiting for a few years until he was eligible for a pension, making me perhaps the first officer with a chauffeur capable of paying my salary. Hierarchies of class and location were, to be sure, getting complicated. Everyone knew Gurgaon was changing. But I did not realize the scale of transformation until I went back, first in 1999 to do research for my previous book, *Virtual Migration*, where I first recognized Gurgaon as a transnational enclave, and then in 2004 when I conducted research for this project. By 2011, the rural periphery had become a global city of 1.5 million people with a literacy rate, 77 percent, higher than the national average of 65 percent. Old Gurgaon is the real periphery now.

We may try to capture this transformation in evolutionary terms from old Gurgaon to new Gurgaon, but it may be advantageous to discount old Gurgaon from our account because it is the least defining, almost distracting, feature of the city, a feature that many in New Gurgaon are only dimly aware of. Gurgaon has not evolved from old to new; it has kept no features of the old. If at all, it is an iteration of a new global template of a city. Unlike old Gurgaon, the new, now real, Gurgaon has no open bazaars; it has only malls. Except for small utility shops in different sectors, there is no city market with street-side shops open to the public; only tightly monitored spaces, nonplaces, of indoor malls where one enters through metal detectors for justifiable safety. It is a variation on a theme-park-like, retail-as-entertainment perspective on consumption.

Sherry Turkle in *Life on the Screen* recalls the anthropologist Ray Oldenberg's writing about the local bar, the bistro, the coffee shop as places of gathering for easy company, conversation, and a sense of belonging. She contrasts this with shopping malls that are entirely planned to maximize purchasing, "On Main Street you are a citizen; in the shopping mall, you are customer as citizen. Main Street had a certain disarray: the town drunk, the traveling snake-oil salesman. The mall is a more controlled space; there may be street theater, but it is planned—the appearance of serendipity is part of the simulation" (Turkle 1995).

This is not an argument against malls per se; in fact, I enjoyed conducting many interviews in a quieter restaurant of Gurgaon's MGF Metropolitan mall. I often took my family from Delhi for a quick weekend trip to Gurgaon's malls where my three-year-old son could run around safe from the unrelenting sun outside (Delhi had not yet developed its own malls). This is also not an argument against functionally differentiated spaces. A conventional city, too, has its specialized zones, its specific neighborhoods, business districts, and specialized markets. My argument relates to a shift from a modernist city of linear development to a city of functional enclaves out-

FIGURE I.7. New Gurgaon

side which things are not so functional. Mini-cities, malls, and corporate parks are all written like programs to perform certain functions; such programs, even if faulty, constitute a city like Gurgaon.

To reduce a city to functionally packaged spaces of consumption, work, and living is to reduce life to interpreted purposes. And everything that does not fit the program is registered as useless noise when urban life is redesigned through formal consumption, when the informal and the unplanned become a sea of chaos surrounding islands of order and function. Ironically, in Gurgaon, the chaos was produced by the very drive to order with few integrative mechanisms in place. Malls brought more traffic than its roads could handle, yet I did not see too many people flocking its shops. Much of the human traffic inside the malls hung around open areas, food courts, cinema halls, and restaurants. I do not remember if I bought anything from their designer shops during my own frequent trips. Prices seemed higher and the shops too specialized (though the emergence of economy-of-scale stores like Big Bazaar might change the situation). People came for relief from heat, traffic, lower classes, and construction chaos that defined the city outside these functionally differentiated spaces. Malls were free from beggars.

Isn't Gurgaon, then, just a familiar story of explosive economic growth? Muffled in concrete and smog, it looks a lot like a conventional city in an economic boom cycle. Cities in the rust belt of the United States, too, rose and declined with the manufacturing sector of the region. What is so special about this urban variation? To add to the earlier story of mini cities, the answer perhaps lies in Gurgaon's development as a city of economic greenhouses, a city of special economic zones (SEZs) where many laws of the national economy stand suspended, reflecting a material reality partly shaped by the globalization of the national state.

## An Archipelago of Transnational Enclaves

The feature that distinguishes Gurgaon from similar examples of growth is the fact of its development as an exception to the rule (Aneesh 2006). Gurgaon has long enjoyed the benefits of India's Exim (export-import) policy relating to export processing zones (EPZs) and software technology parks (STPs) where rules of taxation were suspended in order to promote exports. An SEZ is the latest incarnation of export processing zones, and Gurgaon has a highest number of planned SEZs in the country.

An SEZ is a free trade and warehousing zone, a transnational enclave, that does away with restrictions and regulations governing the national economy. All specified land in SEZs is deemed to be "foreign territory" for the purposes of Indian customs controls, duties, cess, and tariffs.* Thus, special economic zones are exempt from any duty of customs on goods or services imported into or exported from there. There is also no duty of excise on goods brought from Domestic Tariff Area to a Special Economic Zone. Let us take a quick look at the long list of exemptions from national laws (GOI 2005):

- Duty-free import or domestic procurement of goods for development, operation, and maintenance of SEZ units;
- 100 percent Income Tax exemption on export income for SEZ units for first 5 years, 50 percent for next 5 years thereafter and 50 percent of the ploughed back export profit for next 5 years;

---

* "A Special Economic Zone shall, on and from the appointed day, be deemed to be a territory outside the customs territory of India for the purposes of undertaking the authorized operations" (GOI 2005).

- Exemption from minimum alternate tax under section 115JB of the Income Tax Act;
- External commercial borrowing by SEZ units up to US$500 million in a year without any maturity restriction through recognized banking channels;
- Exemption from Central Sales Tax;
- Exemption from Service Tax; Single window clearance for Central and State level approvals;
- Exemption from State sales tax and other levies as extended by the respective State Governments;
- Exemption from customs/excise duties for development of SEZs for operations authorized by the Board of Approval;
- Income Tax exemption on income derived from the business of development of the SEZ in a block of 10 years in 15 years;
- Exemption from dividend distribution tax under Section 115O of the Income Tax Act;
- Exemption from Central Sales Tax; Exemption from Service Tax.

SEZ formation is expected to attract more foreign direct investment, boost exports revenue and provide a global platform for local firms and manufacturers.

In addition, curiously, "Every person, whether employed or residing or required to be present in a Special Economic Zone, shall be provided an identity card by every Development Commissioner of such Special Economic Zone, in such form and containing such particulars as may be prescribed" (GOI 2005). Further, Section 49 of SEZ Act, 2005, authorizes the central government to exempt SEZs from the provisions of any Central Act, including the SEZ Act (other than sections 54 and 56), and any corresponding rules or regulations, meaning SEZs are potentially free from the entire regime of national laws.

Even before the policy of SEZ was enacted, Gurgaon's software firms had enjoyed the status of being export units. New Gurgaon's character depended on software and software-enabled service exports of Rs. 18 thousand crores ($4b USD) a year. The idea of SEZs in India can be traced back to the creation of EPZs, first starting in Kandla (Maharashtra) as far back as 1965. But the idea really took off during the liberalization phase of the 1990s. Quarantined from the domestic tariff area, these were regions where export production was organized on an internationally competitive basis with necessary infrastructure and duty-free imports (Nasscom 2000). Being transnational green-houses, there was no restriction on foreign shareholders in companies that set up units in EPZs and their infrastructure was stipulated to be more dependable, including high-speed data-communication facilities, a more dependable power supply, buildings, and other amenities. Further, a ten-year tax holiday was made available to the units based in EPZs in addition to exemption from income tax on profits derived from the export of software or software-enabled services.

Inefficient management, however, soon started eating into these EPZs, and their performance fell short of expectations. To overcome previous problems, the Special Economic Zones Act, 2005 was passed by Parliament after much discussion and meetings across the country. The SEZ Act, 2005 and SEZ Rules became effective in 2006, defining the key role for the state governments in export promotion and creation of infrastructural facilities. India has more than 1,022 SEZ units currently under the structural formation. It has more than 9 fully functional SEZs and more than 7 EPZs that have been transformed into SEZs. Each of the entirely functional SEZs has a standard dimension of 200 acres; they are spread in different parts of India.

Various features of SEZs give them the image of export-oriented factories rather than urban areas. The layout of an SEZ is divided into a processing area where manufacturing of goods or rendering of services takes place and a nonprocessing area that acts as a support facility with educational institutions, hospitals, hotels, recreational facilities, and residential complexes. An SEZ may specialize in one product or multiple products; it can manufacture goods and render services in a particular sector, e.g., information technology (IT), or it can manufacture goods and services across multiple sectors (multiproduct SEZs). All operational SEZs in Gurgaon—DLF Cyber City, DLF Limited, and Gurgaon Infospace Limited—are focused on IT or IT-enabled services such as call centers. IT and IT-enabled services also form the biggest sector for which SEZs approvals have been granted by the government of India (see figure 1.8). Generally, SEZs are constructed by utilizing an array of institutional compositions varying from complete government-owned organizations to privately owned firms. A Single Window SEZ approval mechanism has been facilitated through a nineteen-member interministerial SEZ Board of Approval or BOA. And the decision of the SEZ Board of Approval is binding and final.

In some cases, the government-owned organizations perform as quasi-government groups in which they follow a pseudocorporate organization

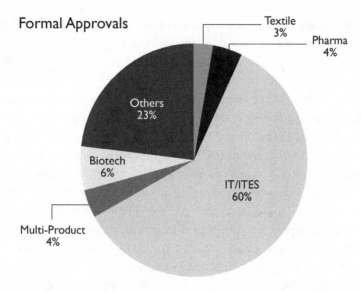

## Formal Approvals

- Textile 3%
- Pharma 4%
- Others 23%
- Biotech 6%
- Multi-Product 4%
- IT/ITES 60%

FIGURE 1.8. SEZ Sectors
*Source:* Government of India: Special Economic Zones in India. www.sezindia.nic.in.

composition and have total control over their budget construction. SEZs are also constructed under the tie-up of private and government organizations where the government sector offers assistance by introducing provisions on infrastructure, investment, and issue of bonds and debentures. This enables the private industry to attain a considerable rate of return on the venture.

Gurgaon, thus, signals an urban variation that has been developing as an exception to the rules that guide national territory. Yet, this exception is developed by the national state itself, revealing what Sassen (2007) calls the crystallization of the global inside the national. Following this strand of urban theory, we can see Gurgaon as an urban formation different from that of the previous era of nationally determined development in India. This denationalization of marked spaces within a city like Gurgaon has changed the historical relationship of mutuality, as pointed out by Taylor (1995), between cities and territorial state, giving rise to new forms of global urbanization. Small wonder, Gurgaon emerges as a global city of a different kind. Unlike New York, Tokyo, and London, Gurgaon has not evolved to be a global city; it is a global city by design. Employing an investor-friendly design to increase foreign direct investment inflows, Gurgaon is less of an evolution of a city, and more of an execution of a plan. The execution might have faltered here and there; it might have distinctly failed on several fronts, but it has decided the character of the city, its layout, its thrills, and its letdowns.

While in the 1990s and early 2000s Gurgaon benefited from the policies that enabled EPZs, its future plans are more ambitious, as the city is "all set to become a separate SEZ country within India with the approval of 52 SEZs, the highest in any district in the country. Nearly 34 per cent of Gurgaon's agricultural land will be covered by these SEZs, and the commercial properties in Gurgaon will be dominated by SEZ properties now and then" (Gonigal 2010). A slew of business conglomerates have ambitious plans for Gurgaon. Reliance Industries Ltd. is setting up India's largest SEZ in Gurgaon, which is projected to have a turnover of US$11 billion in the first year of operation; the company has forged an alliance with Haryana State Industrial Development Corporation (Gonigal 2010). One of the major real estate developers in Gurgaon, DLF, has been given a nod to set up a multiproduct SEZ in Gurgaon on 20,000 acres of land. The company also proposes to demarcate a "free trade zone" within the processing area of the SEZ, which would lay emphasis on trading of goods and commodities manufactured within the SEZ, and the service sector, including BPO, IT, and ITES companies. The private developer will reserve about 2,000 acres for a commercial zone, which will include shops and other establishments such as hotels, office complexes, and banks.

The SEZs in Gurgaon will have residential properties as well. Almost 10,000 acres will be developed exclusively as residential zones, providing all categories of houses for people working in the SEZ. In addition, DLF alone plans to develop about 2,000 to 3,000 acres of land as an institutional area, providing educational, healthcare, and research infrastructure. The multiproduct SEZ would function like a fully integrated city with a separate airport, railway links, including Delhi Metro links, an International Container Depot, and adequate supply of power, water, and communication facilities. DLF (2013) mentions on its website: "Each multi-product SEZ will be developed as an integrated township and will include residential accommodations, commercial and retail facilities, as well as schools, hospitals, hotels and other support infrastructure, including captive power generation facilities."

As I pointed out earlier, current SEZ policies have an ancestry that goes back to SEZ-like policies of the 1980s and 90s when many global software firms and later international call centers mushroomed in Gurgaon, changing its character, pace, and lifestyle. In the wake of corporate influx, the city started attracting thousands of young professionals, who found that living, working, and playing in Gurgaon was cheaper, more convenient, and more fun than in Delhi. As its population knocks up against two million, it has become the biggest hub of India's call centers, where many young college graduates come to work, some as a stopgap measure and others for life.

## Seeking Fortune in Call Centers

Waiting for an interview inside the futuristic building of a major international call center in Gurgaon, I struck up a conversation in the lobby with Chandra, a forty-three-year-old man, who had applied for a job as a calling agent. He was waiting to be interviewed by a manager. A mechanical engineer by training, Chandra had been tutoring kids in math to earn a monthly income of Rs. 20–25,000 at the rate of Rs. 200–250 an hour in New Delhi. Of late, his salary had gone down to Rs. 8000, he complained, because of the wage-depressing competition from migrants who increasingly came from Bihar—one of the poorest states in India—and who were ready to tutor at the meager rate of Rs. 50 an hour. With a family to fend for, he was left with no choice except to apply for a customer-care job at the age of forty-three with an embarrassing prospect of working alongside youngsters in their early twenties. Little did Chandra realize that if he got the position of customer-care agent, he would himself become a migrant of a virtual kind (Aneesh 2006), contributing to a similar debate of wage depression in the United States through outsourcing to Indian call centers.

To Chandra's dismay, call centers were already flooded with migrants from the states of Bihar, Uttar Pradesh, and even the south. Narayan was one of them. At the age of twenty-four, the wide-eyed Narayan was a far better hire for any call center. He was younger and driven, more capable of grueling night shifts. Chandra was rejected by the call center on a technical basis: he was born before their cutoff year of 1970. I am not sure how many call centers followed the explicit criterion of age in their hiring practices (GoCom did hire older folks) but the bias toward the young on both demand and supply sides was crystal clear to anyone who ever visited a call center.

Narayan came to Gurgaon in the winter of 2001 when those beguiling mornings, dipped in the smog-filled blue haze, reminded him, ironically, of a hill station. Clearly, the smell of petrol fumes did not point a back-to-nature retreat; instead, it signaled an advance, a sign of the future full of progress. Moving from Kanpur, a north Indian city in long decline, now an unruly mockery of its industrial past, Narayan showed an unusual degree of optimism about his life in Gurgaon, the only agent among my interviewees who planned to make their call center work a lifelong career.

Narayan was unlike any other agent I knew: he came from a family of call center agents. His mother worked at a domestic call center in his hometown, Kanpur, and was recently promoted to floor manager. His sister moved with him and worked for another call center in Okhla, a neighborhood in New Delhi. After completing a bachelor's degree in commerce, Narayan did not suffer from the anguish that afflicted other agents about their career. Most others considered their call center stints as an easy means for quick money, a stopgap arrangement as they prepared for their MBA entrance test or other exams and waited for the results; it was a resting place before they journeyed to greener pastures. Narayan was different. He was on leave from another call center, trying it out at GoCom for a month to evaluate if the salary promised in newspaper ads was the real deal. Unlike others, the decision to work in the call center industry was not agonizing for him. Initially, he failed to get a position in an international call center, and worked in a domestic call center for NIIT in Kanpur before coming to Gurgaon. He took the job seriously and disapproved of other agents' frivolous attitude toward call center work.

"You know what people do?" he said. "They just do a time pass. Here in Gurgaon or in Delhi. I know that people are doing the job not for their necessity, they are doing job for fashion . . . for pocket money. For Kanpur people [like himself], it is not a time-pass or fashion, it is their life. If you are serious about your job then you can achieve anything." Narayan recounted how difficult it was for him and his sister to leave their family, but they did it for this job. "I was living with my parents," Narayan recounted, ". . . when I was coming from Kanpur to Delhi, you know, they were just crying; they said you are going, and that is very, very good; but they do not think that anytime soon [they will live together again]; they just want to live with me." Narayan seemed a typical, starry-eyed migrant: missing home, yet brimming with energy and impatience to build a future.

But the transition was not smooth. Like most migrants, Narayan was persistently critical of the new place, remembering his life in Kanpur with wistful fondness. Places of arrival tend to fall short of the dream. Gurgaon could never compete with Narayan's nostalgia, which accentuated the felt disjunctures of Gurgaon. Yet one could also read in his nostalgia for Kanpur a longing for a life that had felt more real, unlike what it had of late become: a series of performances in someone else's play. His life now was full of conversations, as he fielded 200–300 calls a night; yet he could only imagine the person at the other end. Lacking an access to British or American cultures where his respondents were located, he could "know" them only in his own terms, or more precisely, in terms taught by the company, transforming them in the process. In fact, he had barely gained access to Gurgaon, the city of his employment, where the language of social life was different from that of Kanpur. Although unlike others he regarded his career in call centers as permanent, he showed no interest, when I asked, in settling down in Gurgaon. "No, no. You know," he replied, "here in Gurgaon and Delhi, the money is very, very good, but I have been feeling . . . you cannot live here because money can come, feelings cannot." He added, if you asked for directions in Gurgaon, for instance, people in Gurgaon may give you wrong directions, "but in Kanpur, they just say, okay sit on my scooter, and I will drop you off." The behavior of people in Gurgaon was a jarring change from what he was used to in Kanpur.

While he may be disappointed at the lack of desired sociability in Gurgaon, he could try to understand the logic of the new city. At least, he expected a bigger city to be much more impersonal. But his understanding of America and Britain was largely based on imagination, signifying a second set of felt disjunctures: a chasm of India and America now existing simultaneously in his waking life. He thought that call center agents in the United States were higher level workers. He ruminated, "So if I open an International call center in America, then I have to pay Rs. 120,000 for a person [i.e., $3,000 a month in 2005], and for the meal, I have to provide Five Star Hotel meal, and I have to provide full accommodation. For a pick-up and drop-off facility, I have to provide a car, and there telecasting is very, very high, very, very expensive compared to India. That's why people come here in India, and they just open their call centers." Of course, Narayan could ruminate about call centers in the United States only in terms of the frame available to him. It would not occur to him that American call centers did not provide meals, let alone five-star hotel meals; that unlike India, the food in five-star hotels in the United States was not known to be good; that they did not pick up or drop off their employees at their homes; and that most of their employees earned a meager $10 an hour at the time. While serving his American clients and living transnationally in American time zones, Narayan remained quite palpably in Gurgaon, which, despite being connected on a constant basis to the United States, also remained deeply disconnected.

Gurgaon is thus a city of many enclaves, persistently connected and disconnected, an inscrutable, even surreal city—a city of mini cities with a fondness for walled gardens, private security, and programmed fun. No longer is it a local city where people's identity is connected to the region's history and its community but a global city in the service of a virtualized global society. Whole fields of green have vanished from Gurgaon's memory, countless fertile farms never to be visited again, all transformed into an archipelago of transnational enclaves, simultaneously hitched and unhitched to its surrounds. There is nothing more emblematic of the rapid transformation of the city than its call centers. We shall enter one of them in chapter 2.

Inside a Call Center: *Otherworldly Passages*

It was half past midnight. GoCom floors were all bustle and hum. Many agents and their team leaders were at work. A few others were in the cafeteria, in short queues; men and women went about getting food on steel plates with separate compartments for daal, rice, vegetables, raita, and a small one for the pickle. There was, in general, much loading and unloading of food. Kitchen managers collected food coupons from agents ceaselessly, making sure that no one picked up more dessert than the coupon's worth.

There was nothing out of the ordinary about the cafeteria except for one crucial detail: agents were having lunch after midnight. They slept during the day and began work in the evening. One could see how separate registers were bound together: the body's diurnal hardwiring was adjusting to a nocturnal diet, GoCom's agents were connecting live with the United States and United Kingdom while Gurgaon slept quietly outside the business district, and the trainees learned work processes and practiced accents and cultural performances for people they never knew, and places they would never see. It took me a week getting used to sleeping in the day and having lunch and dessert around midnight.

I slowly realized what I had only intellectually understood. GoCom, like other international call centers, was driven by programs of another world. Its daily rhythms to a considerable extent were determined by rhythms of other places. Indeed, the entire night economy of Gurgaon's call centers was tied to the days of other places. The feverish nighttime rush of call center taxicabs was determined by the work hours of Seattle or London or Sydney. And all international call centers with thousands of workers might be operating in time zones of other places. Enchanting as it may seem, the night economy of Gurgaon is not the same as the night economy of Las Vegas. Unlike Vegas, nights of Gurgaon are hitched, directly and unavoidably, to the days of other places.

Located in Udyog Vihar in Gurgaon where many software and service firms are based, GoCom specialized in telemarketing services, mostly pertaining to mobile phone connections, for clients based in the United Kingdom and United States. Inside GoCom, there were three major areas of activities: at the lower level were classrooms for training in foreign cultures, accents, and work processes; at the ground level was the cafeteria for lunch and snacks where the trainees and the trained rubbed shoulders, and on the top floor live calls to overseas customers were made by seasoned agents. While classrooms were located in the basement, closeted away from local influences, the floor—the sacred space for global calling—occupied the top floor above office din and in immediate touch with clients and customers abroad. There were tea and coffee machines installed in multiple places on the ground floor. A large open terrace, separated by a wall of glass, was put quickly to use by young smokers—all in their twenties—whose number surprised me. Indian middle-class families generally have strong sanctions against smoking.

Compared to my experience at Datys, where I failed to get the voice and accent trainer's position after three interviews, it was easier to get an ordinary agent's job at GoCom, where the interview was over in ten minutes and I was hired along with many others. I was asked to show up next week to get the formal letter of employment and start my training. The training at GoCom was not as rigorous as it was at other, more prestigious call centers such as Convergys or Daksha, or so I was told by more experienced agents. I immediately took a liking to the group I was training with. Some of them conveyed with gallows humor the utter desperation of telemarketing work.

"Mr. Anderson, I'll do anything if you accept this amazing offer," Baveja offered us advice about how to make a sale. Armed with sufficient work experience at another call center, he continued, clearing his throat and putting on a fake accent, "I'll eat your shit, sir, if you just buy this bloody thing." He was cheered by a collective nervous laughter.

In his own way, Baveja expressed the paradox of connection and disconnection. While one was connected to an actual person overseas, there was a clear recognition of disconnection. Although Baveja knew that the person at the other end was real, requiring honesty in conversation, it was easy for him to offer fake respect without liability because despite the pretense of conversation, the customer on the phone remained a construct of his training and imagination, allowing him to focus only on the objectives of business. To his overseas customers, Baveja himself was merely a racial type with a strange accent from another world, deserving suspicion, not respect. Their encounter would feel like a game of simulation where the parties perceived the other through multiple screens. Yet it was the agent—not the customer—who was more aware of the game. After all, the agent was working for the organization, the call center, which was a major actor in the global game. Expectedly, agents were less suspicious of the customer; their distrust was directed more against their employer, the call center, whose dealings with their overseas contracting companies felt murky. The customer's ire, on the other hand, was often directed against the agent because there was no way for the customer to know if and what Indian call center serviced their bank, credit card company, or phone company. Their reach was limited to the agent whose transnational character was beyond full grasp and therefore dubious and suspect.

## Suspect Behavior

Having met and interviewed many employees in my career, I found that call center agents, unlike employees in other industries, showed a lot less pride and loyalty for their companies in general. At GoCom, I noticed an utter disregard, even contempt, for call center operations, their profit, and their motives. Employees wanted to know how much money they were making for their company through telemarketing, for instance; but the knowledge of GoCom's dealings with its UK- and U.S.-based clients did not trickle down to its employees, who always kept guessing the profits the company made on their shoulders. With a typical Indian trait, agents often gave their conjectures an air of certainty.

"They are making huge profits," Mukul claimed. Referring to GoCom's telemarketing campaign for its UK-based client selling mobile phone connections to Londoners, he went on to calculate their profits quite meticulously, "Ok, for one hundred and sixty people [working the process on the floor], he's asking for two forty applications a day [only completed customer applications counted as sales]. . . . It means in thirty days, five days are off, it comes to 6,000 sales. They are just looking for 6,000 sales and just look at the amount of money they should be earning from it." Mukul did not stop at the company's estimated profits, he suspected GoCom of cheating employees out of their incentive-based income.

"I gave out nine sales . . . and the report came to just six sales, five were dispatched, no return, one was sale with complaints," Mukul continued, "But three sales, I don't know where they went . . . I asked Joshi [team leader] what happened to the three sales? I told them the names [and they said] Ok, ok, we shall look into that."

"They can't just take the sales away from you," I expressed with incredulity. Mukul responded plainly, "No, they may be going into someone else's account." He accepted his situation with saintly humor, "Ok, someone is benefiting even if I am not going to get incentives for all the nine sales." He went on to a fuller exegesis of the company's suspect behavior.

"What I've come to know about this company is that everything happens through the back door . . . even if you are performing, even if you are making fifty plus sales, the company is saying ok, ten were returned. You can't do nothing. You don't have any proof with you. . . . There was a guy who said he made about 30–40 sales. The company told him it was only fourteen . . . the rest were returned. . . . They may be true, maybe they also lie, he's not sure. So you can't do anything. The company is benefiting . . . the guy was supposed to get incentive of Rs. 30,000 he was just getting 15 or 14 because of huge returns this time." Was there any way for the person to know that they were actual returns or the company was just lying?

"How can you know?" Mukul replied. "You will never have physical proof of it. You just have a paperless contract . . . Even if they say this customer has returned, and you call the customer, the person says I am using it. How do you know that the customer is lying or not?"

The suspicion about GoCom's motives and management ran deep and wide. Perhaps it was not completely unfounded. Even during my short stint I noticed deception, if not outright cheating, regarding the promise of salary. It was only a minor instance of false advertising, but it did point to issues highlighted by Mukul. In 2005, the way the job was advertised, I thought my monthly salary would be close to Rs. 20,000 (US$400 at the time) but once hired, I was surprised along with a few others to notice that my base salary was quite low, Rs. 7000 (US$150) to be precise. The letter of intent noted that "Pursuant to our meeting, we are pleased to make you an Offer, as sales officer at our office in Gurgaon. You will be entitled to a package of Rs. 20,200. However, the complete details of your compensation package will be stated in the letter of appointment, which will be served to you on your joining our organization." But when I joined I was given a document with the breakup of my salary as follows:

- Base salary: 7,000 (7th of every month. Take home Salary after PF and TDS deduction);
- Expected Performance level (EPL): 15 sales; Performance: 6,000 (EPL+4 sales=Rs. 3,000; EPL+8 sales=6,000);
- Loyalty: 2,000 (After 6 months Rs. 12,000 will be due, payable in the month of 7th, 8th, 9th, 10th: Eligibility: 90% of EPL);
- Transport & Cafeteria; 4,200 (Have to avail these facilities, cost of the facilities); Attendance: 1,000 (21st–25th of every month. No unscheduled leave (sick leave is unscheduled));
- CTC pm: Rs. 20,200.

The initial package seemed to have mostly evaporated. There was no incentive attached to first fifteen sales, which to my mind was all one could think of making in realistic terms. Unachievable incentives marred the compensation package.

Small wonder no agent thought that call centers were doing something worthwhile, let alone anything good for society. And we cannot blame the agents for their lack of respect for their employers. At GoCom, I was informed by Vikas about something called "bhasad" accounts, sales made by deliberately misleading the customer. Under the pressure of unachievable incentive-based income, agents were driven to the same kind of deception that they suspected GoCom to be engaged in. Tactics of deception were adopted with minimal sense of consequence partly because the overseas customer remained mostly an abstract customer and the agent assumed himself to be out of reach if the customer uncovered the deception. Although GoCom was contractually obligated to follow country-specific consumer protection laws available to the customer, in this case British customers, it was their client, a UK company, in the end, that needed to make sure that British laws were being respected by their Indian subcontractor. The agent was at a remove from the customer, legally, physically, and culturally.

Bhasad accounts, according to Vikas, were created by either promising the customer something that wasn't possible or speaking the fine print of an offer so fast that the customer couldn't hear it to make an informed decision. Mukul gave a fuller exposition by explaining how manual dialing involves some nonrecorded lines, lines that one could use to make semitrue promises.

"You can say anything," Mukul explained, "you can say after fourteen days [the customer] can return it [mobile connection and the cell phone]. You can say anything . . . Roaming is free, international roaming is free. It's a scam . . . as long as the customer is holding on to that . . . you can do anything." On the basis of free promises, the customer was encouraged to say "yes," when transferred to the manager who registered her agreement with the paperless contract. In a separate interview, Sanjay confirmed the strategy of "free stuff" employed by the agents.

"We are allowed to say it's not a sales call, we're not selling you anything," Sanjay described. "They start the call like this . . . hi my name is this and I'm calling with this company. From now onward, all your calls will be absolutely free . . . And then afterward I can say that this is a plan, this is how much you have to pay and all your calls will be free . . . you are getting this free in-car charger, free in-car holder along with this . . . phone connection. Free this, free that, free talk time. You know, Americans like freebies. When they hear free things, they probably don't hang up on you."

"It's not good," Mukul showed ethical disapproval, "I talked to a customer. He said he was never going to take a free connection, he took it from another agent and was promised a free phone but they never got the cash back, they never got free text messaging . . . he was being charged more for that." Agents may not explain to the customer, for instance, the company policy about the cash back, that "it takes about one or two months for you to get it" only if the customer mailed them the first bill within fourteen days. The company doesn't "encourage you to tell the customer" everything in clear terms, Mukul said, "only if he [the customer] asks what the procedure is to get the cash, you can say you have to send so and so bill to the customer care." Often, the agent didn't inform, Mukul noted, about the deadline by which the customer was supposed to send it.

Mukul was the only agent at GoCom who had migrated from southern India, from the state called Kerala, instead of joining a call center at a closer location like Bangalore. Unlike his colleagues, his motivation to work for a call center was neither a stopgap arrangement until he got a better job nor was it for quick money. The job aided his pursuit of a married woman he fell in love with during a trip to Chad in Africa as a trade manager for his company. He left a better paying job as a foreign trade manager in southern India to work in the north where there was no family to pressure him into marriage, and no family to watch him agonize over his girlfriend who now lived with her husband in Gurgaon. He may have been unconventional at heart, but he took his job more seriously than most of his colleagues.

Mukul gave another example of an agent who told the customer "your contract is due to expire," to which the customer responded, "no, my contract is not expiring." It didn't work in that particular case, but Mukul was aware that this falsehood was a frequently used line of opening in this telemarketing campaign; he explained, "UK people don't know when their contract is expiring." So they are prone to renewing it before it's due, fetching GoCom its business and the agent his incentive. "Some people don't even know how much [they are paying], then after six months they come to know, ok, this is what I am being debited."

While agents did not openly flout the laws and regulations of the countries they were serving, their connection with those laws was tenuous by default. It wasn't so long ago that they had memorized the laws. Quite like their customers, the laws were distant and difficult to relate to.

### Abiding by the Laws of Another Land

The agent was at a remove from the laws of other countries but was required to learn them, nonetheless. Call center work was defined by the knowledge of laws and places with which they had no direct contact, no immediate relationship.

"We read a lot about regulations and laws, not only read, crammed them up," Geeta noted, "every day I used to come back and study . . . You come to know a lot . . . [how] credit card holders [are] fully protected by every CPA. Even if you owe a lot of money to me as a lender or bank, the collection agency cannot harass you, when I call you, the phone cannot ring more than ten times. And if you say, 'do not call,' I cannot call you again, and ask you for the money." Geeta's and her colleagues in debt collection processes had committed to memory such American laws as Fair Debt Collection Practices Act, including their various sections, as reflected by her notes in figure 2.1.

Surprising as it may seem, the laws of another country furnished better information, if only indirectly, about its culture than the month-long train-

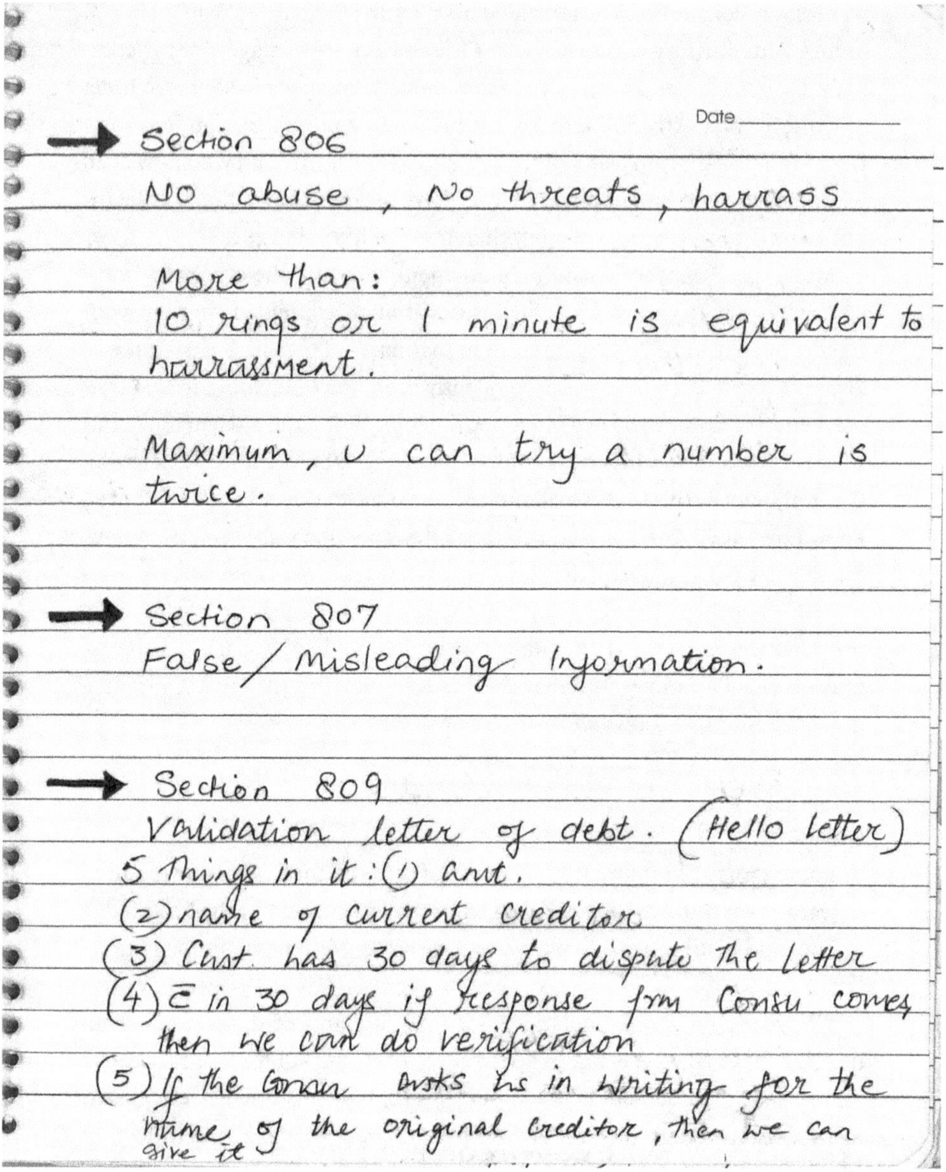

→ Section 806

NO abuse , No threats , harrass

More than:
10 rings or 1 minute is equivalent to
harrassment.

Maximum, u can try a number is
twice.

→ Section 807
False / Misleading Information.

→ Section 809
Validation letter of debt. (Hello letter)
5 Things in it : (1) amt.
(2) name of current creditor.
(3) Cust has 30 days to dispute the letter
(4) c̄ in 30 days if response frm Consu comes
then we can't do verification
(5) If the Consu asks us in writing for the
name of the original creditor, then we can
give it

FIGURE 2.1. Laws from abroad

ing in culture did. Debt collection, for instance, was a major component of many call centers. But the rules and regulations of debt collection were a matter of cultural curiosity among the agents. A process from another world, Geeta found it intriguing that debt was such a private issue in the United States. Agents were required to follow strict norms of privacy and understand a different way of relating with others.

Even when the customer says, "Don't bother me about the amount, talk to my attorney," Geeta recalled, "and the attorney calls up, and says, yeah I'm calling on behalf of Aneesh, I'm his attorney," she had to treat the attorney as a "third party." She was required to "ask him to send a letter in writing to say he is representing you . . . because it is your personal information, I cannot let even your spouse know in certain states. Or even your parents know, or anybody at work, anyone except you. You are the right party to contact. I can only tell you about it, discuss it with you. In certain states, I can discuss with your wife also." Geeta joked that here in the state of Haryana if you owe someone money and don't pay it back, you may have to answer to you know who—the local goonda—and everyone in your family would quickly come to know of your debt.

Indian families are conservative borrowers with a strong cultural aversion to loans. Despite a recent rise in outstanding credit card debt, delinquency rates are relatively low across Asia, and India's household debt was 10 percent of GDP compared to the United States's 83 percent in 2012 (The Economist 2012). About half of Americans have more credit card debt than in emergency savings, according to a 2013 survey (Bankrate 2013).

For agents engaged in collection, both debt and directives for handling default were matters of fascination. Making collection calls was a form of tourism where one came to know the everyday foreign culture more than one does during a visit to Niagara Falls or a Vegas casino (without the fun). Sitting in Gurgaon, Geeta had to convince the people who defaulted on their debt to pay up, "convince them in a very kind manner, like friends; we cannot demand from them; because of all these CPA laws and because we really have to counsel them and convince them that how this is such a good plan, we can break up your payment, we will waive off a certain amount . . . We tell them, see, we will help you with installments, once you pay off, your credit rating will go up and you will get a better loan, a mortgage." It is remarkable that Geeta had learned the meaning of credit rating and what it did to a person's economic well-being in the United States. In India, there was no credit score for the individual, at least not yet, that could reflect a person's worth.

Geeta in her early 40s was an outsider in an industry where 50 percent of employees were under twenty-five years of age (Nasscom 2011). Having worked in three high profile call centers, she turned out to be a key informant who shared with me bundles of class notes taken on various training sites and sessions. Considerate and caring, Geeta told me her poignant life story. Her husband had left her for a younger woman, managing to take both the kids along with him to another part of India. Despite being a college graduate, it was not easy for her to be a divorcée living with her parents, partly because divorces were not common in the social circle of her influential, though conservative, family. In a long interview at her house in Gurgaon, she interspersed her views of the call center industry with details of her family life. The two were connected. Being abandoned by her husband led her to an easier-to-get call center job. While night work takes a toll on one's social life, it was convenient given her life circumstances. She could sleep her way out of the daytime hubbub and gossip of her family social circle in Gurgaon. It was a good way to hide. With no work experience in any other industry but with fluency in English, call centers were a perfect match.

"Initially I got selected for collections at GE," she recounted her difficulties when she worked for GE Capital. "I didn't study. I went south to meet my kids. My family told [me] not to tell my kids who would tell their father, and that's why I didn't want them to know [that I was working]. [Otherwise] I won't get my maintenance [alimony]. That's why I didn't carry my books also. As soon I came back, I came from the airport straight to the office, and I failed the test, I couldn't clear the test." Eventually, she moved to another call center and then another.

Much as the agent learned and memorized the laws, rules, and regulations of another country, there were always failures of understanding. The scholastic entrance into another world tended to be narrow and full of blind spots. They may have gained a basic understanding of credit rating and mortgage system but failed at times to understand some basic terms.

"I had absolutely no idea what a jumbo loan was," Tarun, who worked on home loans, noted. "That was the second or third day of my calling. I give him a call [and ask], do you have a swimming pool in your backyard, or if you would like to have a driveway, and [he asks] do you also give jumbo loans? I was taken aback. At that moment I was about to make a sale, the fellow gave me a crack at it, and I had absolutely no idea [what a jumbo loan was]. And I am supposed to be the expert in that field." A college graduate from Patna, Tarun was outspoken, gregarious, and funny. He was proud of the fact that he learned English on his own. As a teenager, he could hardly speak any English. Once he heard two guys cracking jokes in English in his neighborhood, "I also wanted to crack a joke . . . but the moment I started trying to speak this language of yours, if I may say so, . . . they just chuckled at me and said yep and . . . that hurt me a lot." After that incident, "I said, fine, all right. I'll watch all the funny movies they have made . . . and I'll get damn good at English . . . I had this small television of mine. I got it connected with the cable TV, and I purchased a lot of books. I read a lot of books. I think it took me two years." Soon he moved to New Delhi and found himself working at a call center, speaking English every night and learning overseas laws and regulations.

I was surprised to notice the agent's awareness of the minor rules and regulations that were foreign to them. Mini Miranda, for instance, was an interesting rule that all debt collection agents were required to say at the beginning of a call. It is a warning system mandated by the U.S. Fair Debt Collection Practices Act, which demands that all debt collection calls and correspondence must carry an advisement that the call or letter is from a debt collector and is for the purpose of collecting a debt and that any information obtained from the debtor will be used for that purpose. This is an important legal right against debt collectors who threaten, harass, call at odd hours, or make false representations to the debtor. For the collector, the rule was a nuisance. Ranjana noted, "There is a thing called Mini-Miranda, which you have to state. When we start with it they hang up or they start abusing, because they have figured out that it is just a collections call. There are so many rules in the United States, you have to follow them."

Ebullient and sharp, Ranjana had an eye for catching ironies that seem to afflict call centers more than any other organization. Having worked mostly in collection-oriented processes, she was amused to note that she collected even from the dead.

"Some people have died, like already three years back, and we are still making collection calls," she remembered, "The person is dead and the wife is not ready to pay, saying that it is not my loan, why should I pay?" Ranjana chuckled to highlight more ironies of collection, noting how she spent her precious time collecting amounts like a dollar, "The $1 thing . . . they have this whole list that comes on the screen and you see $1, $3, and you feel funny asking for it . . . There was this man who said I am going to pay it in installments, I was so struck, like what installments? Some Americans have a nice sense of humor, I should say. I will pay it in installment . . . You go like, 'okay.'" Humor aside, Ranjana wasn't too happy with the job.

"One day I just got up from the chair and said I am leaving, and I walked out. The HR person tried to convince me, brainwash me that no, you should stay. I wanted to quit. I got really fed up." Ranjana did have a place to go, though. She had been accepted at a master's program at Jawaharlal Nehru University.

In addition to the laws, agents also juggled different geographies. I was impressed by their knowledge of geographical details of the countries they were serving. During my training, I realized that a few agents were already better at answering many quiz questions about the United States than I was. Geeta along with others had memorized the capitals of all the fifty states of the United States of America. To make sure she pronounced the names correctly, she jotted down in her native Hindi, a highly phonetic script, the correct pronunciation of the names that the English script rendered ambiguous. For example, she made sure that she did not mispronounce Wichita as Wikita, that "ch" there is not as in chemistry but as in charcoal.

During a break between training sessions, I realized that more than half the trainees had already worked for another call center. They had just switched to GoCom from another call center. No wonder some of them could list all the fifty states of America more quickly than I could. Still, they showed respect for my having lived in the United States, a country of constant fascination.

When Vikas started to work for a call center, he was surprised to know that the United States used more than twenty types of street designations from Boulevards to Alleys to Drives, each with its own acronym. In his new identity as "Victor," he needed to know the format of American address to which he was introduced during training, as shown in figure 2.3.

The above street designations, not used in India, were committed to memory, serving a dual purpose: Vikas could keep the persona of Victor without fumbling over ordinary terms, and he could perform his job with ease. This preparation also allowed agents to understand urban America and offered customers such ordinary services as driving directions.

"When a person calls up . . . ," Geeta illustrated how she could guide a customer to a location in the United States when she worked for Datys, which served Citibank from Gurgaon, "we say welcome to the Citibank . . . and ask them what we can do for you . . . They would probably say I didn't

मन-गा श्री

| | States | State Codes | Capital Cities | Important Cities |
|---|---|---|---|---|
| 1 | Alabama | AL | Montgomery (mn-GUM-ree) | Birmingham (BER-ming-ham), Mobile (mo-BEEL) |
| 2 | Alaska | AK | Juneau (JU-noo) जुनी | इसँ > इसाँ |
| 3 | Arizona | AZ | Phoenix | Tucson, Scottsdale |
| 4 | Arkansas अरिकनसा | AR | Little Rock लिलर | Pine Bluff, Hot Springs |
| 5 | California | CA | Sacramento | Los Angeles, San Francisco, San Diego |
| 6 | Colorado | CO | Denver | Vail, Aspen |
| 7 | Connecticut | CT | Hartford | |
| 8 | Delaware | DE | Dover | |
| 9 | District of Columbia | DC | Washington D.C. | |
| 10 | Florida | FL | Tallahassee | Orlando, Miami, Ft Lauderdale FoRT |
| 11 | Georgia | GA | Atlanta | |
| 12 | Hawaii | HI | Honolulu | |
| 13 | Idaho अिहाइ डो | ID | Boise  BOISEE  BOIZEE | |
| 14 | Illinois | IL | Springfield | Chicago, Peoria (pE-'Or-E▲A) |
| 15 | Indiana | IN | Indianapolis INDNAPLIS | Gary, Bloomington, Valparaiso (val-p▲-'rEE")zO |
| 16 | Iowa अिय औ व | IA | Des Moines दू औियन | Cedar Rapids |
| 17 | Kansas | KS | Topeka टेपीका | Kansas City, Wichita विचिटी |
| 18 | Kentucky केन टकी | KY | Frankfort | Louisville, Lexington लुइ विलन |
| 19 | Louisiana | LA | Baton Rouge बेटन रूझ | New Orleans, Shreveport श्रीव पोर्ट |
| 20 | Maine | ME | Augusta | |
| 21 | Mary Land | MD | Annapolis ANNAPLIS | |
| 22 | Massachusetts | MA | Boston बोस्टन | |
| 23 | Michigan | MI | Lansing | Detroit, Pontiac ('pän-tE-"ak) , Ann Arbor अैनआर अैन आरबर |
| 24 | Minnesota | MN | St. Paul | |
| 25 | Mississippi | MS | Jackson | Vicksburg |
| 26 | Missouri मिसुरी | MO | Jefferson City | St. Louis |

20

FIGURE 2.2. States of the United States

## Street Designations

| | | | |
|---|---|---|---|
| ✧HEIGHTS | ✧HTS | ✧RIDGE | ✧RDG |
| ✧MANOR | ✧MNR | ✧ROUTE | ✧RTE |
| ✧MALL | ✧MALL | ✧SHOAL | |
| ✧MEADOW | ✧MDW | ✧SQUARE | ✧SQ |
| ✧MOTORWAY | ✧MTWY | ✧STREET | ✧ST |
| ✧MOUNTAIN | ✧MTN | ✧TERRACE | ✧TRC/TER |
| ✧ORCHARD | ✧ORCH | ✧ TURNPIKE | ✧TRNPK |
| ✧PARKWAY | ✧PKWY | ✧VALLEY | ✧VLY |
| ✧PRAIRIE | ✧PR | ✧VILLE | |
| ✧PLAZA | ✧PLZ | ✧VISTA | |
| ✧RANCH | ✧ RNCH | | |
| ✧RAPID | ✧RPD | | |

## Street Designations

| | | | |
|---|---|---|---|
| ✧ALLEY | ✧ALY | ✧ARCADE | ✧ARC |
| ✧BAYOO | ✧BYU | ✧FLAT | ✧FLT |
| ✧BOULEVARD | ✧BLVD | ✧FOREST | ✧FRST |
| ✧BYPASS | ✧BYP | ✧FREEWAY | ✧FWY/FRWY |
| ✧CANYON | ✧CYN | ✧GARDEN | ✧GDN |
| ✧CIRCLES | ✧CIR | ✧GATEWAY | ✧GTWY |
| ✧CREEK | ✧CRK | ✧GROVE | ✧GRV |
| ✧CRESCENT | ✧CRES/ CREST/ CRST | ✧HARBOR | ✧HBR |
| ✧CROSSING | ✧XING | ✧HAVEN | ✧HVN |
| ✧DRIVE | ✧DR | ✧HIGHWAY | ✧HWY |
| ✧ESTATE | ✧EST | ✧ISLAND | ✧ISL |
| ✧EXTENSIONS | ✧EXT | ✧JUNCTION | ✧JCT |
| ✧ISLE | | ✧LANE | ✧LN |

FIGURE 2.3. Street designations

get my statement this month, or my spouse or friend or relative has spent the money, where it was spent, on which date, or they are new in the area, and they might say "where is your closest branch? We would say OK, where are you? What's the zip code of your place? The closest ones in that area would come up [appear on the screen]; along with the bus route, train route, landmarks along the way, we can easily guide them to that place."

But such tools and training often failed when basic cultural understanding was required. The problem of cultural distance, more than physical distance, plagues all global conversations, which depend only on aural cues without physical interaction. When the two parties have entirely different experiential bases, the potential for "pragmatic failure" in global communication increases greatly. Pragmatic failure implies the inability to understand "what is meant by what is said" (Thomas 1984). The likelihood of sociopragmatic failure, which involves one's social experiences and system of beliefs as much as one's knowledge of language (Thomas 1984), was a constant risk. While it was possible for Geeta in Gurgaon to provide navigational information to her American customers through interactive map software, a simple question requiring an understanding of American urban culture could unsettle the ongoing communication. When Tarun was asked how many blocks away was their Citibank office from a certain intersection, he failed to understand the very meaning of "blocks."

"We do not have any idea what exactly they measure by blocks," Tarun noted, "two blocks away, three blocks away, and things like that. We know mohallas. You talk about mohallas, we are three mohallas away from you, how many chowks are there in your area . . . I asked my TL [team leader] what exactly they mean by two blocks away? He said, you say, I'm four blocks away; nobody gives a damn." Major Indian cities are not designed in rectangular blocks, an essential feature of urban culture in the United States.

Just as cultural tourism is a reminder of cultural distance, agents were acutely aware through repeated interactions of their separation from the crowd they were trying to serve.

"Convincing a person sitting in Delhi in the middle of the night to pay off his credit card bills in the United States is a very hard thing," Tarun observed. Unlike cultural tourism and its noninstrumental symbolic consumption, agents navigated other cultures through deeply purposive, and therefore, exhaustive work. Telemarketing, in particular, is demanding by nature, being infected with constant rejection.

"Emotionally thinking, [telemarketing] is just like begging," Sanjay ruminated, "you know, when you call up, they talk to you like how you treat beggars here." Sanjay was a serious man in his twenties. When he first joined a call center—he had worked in eight by the time I met him—he was fascinated by everything American. But now he appeared a little disillusioned. He thought of readjusting his attitude toward beggars, "Up till then, I was such an ignorant person. I used to think this beggar [on the street] was bothering me. But it was not the beggar who was bothering me, there is just someone who's handling these beggars," referring to the local mob or street entrepreneurs who organize street begging in India just as call centers organized their own performance of begging. Perhaps, comparing telemarketing and begging is a stretch, but most of the telemarketing calls, like begging, did not materialize in sales. Pressures of telemarketing and of culture work were enough for agents on the floor to look fondly back at the training period as the honeymoon period.

At GoCom, our training period ended within a month, and we were moved to the floor, first to barge in on live calls and then to make calls. Our training period was far shorter than what it may have been in more established call centers, where voice and accent training could go on for a couple of months. Suddenly, we shifted from the training culture of long breaks, coffee, and tea to the floor of no breaks and ceaseless calling.

## This Worldly Regimen

"Let me tell you another thing," Geeta recalled working at Datys and serving Citibank customers. "What happens is that in Citibank you've got your headset on, you've got the screen there, you are sitting like that and this phone comes, it just goes tittttting, when that happens you have to immediately start talking, OK, and as soon as you finish with the call, and you press release. You barely finish pressing the release, and it goes titting again." The dialer did not give any breaks between calls. Even the scheduled breaks were hard to come by.

"If you need that little bit of break [that] is scheduled," Geeta ruminated, "you have to log on, asking for the system's assistance for the break, and you think you will get it now, you will get it now, one hour will pass, two hours will pass, three hours will pass, those calls will not stop coming, and the system will not be able to get you a break on the floor." When "the call flow" was "heavy," she was "not allowed to hang up on a customer."

"What if you have to go to the bathroom or something," I asked.

"Yeah, it's difficult," she responded, "and what happened at Citibank I stopped having my dinner; for me, it was dieting but on the other hand, I thought I would rather go and have a smoke; when you are tired you need a break." Geeta preferred working at Keane where "in nine hours" she got "twenty-five minutes . . . for dinner, and before that sometime in the first half we get fifteen minutes for a coffee break; you can go to the washroom. But at [Datys] they would not allow us, we had the same timing but if you wanted to go to the washroom and all, it was not [easy]."

It took our group three weeks to move from GoCom's basement classrooms where training was conducted to the hallowed grounds of the *floor* where one made live calls. I remember the feeling of awe and dread when we were taken there for mock calls at first. An uneasy silence marked our passage into a room located in one corner of a large open hall from whose glass walls we could see but not hear the action on the floor. A wide open hall was divided up into open cubicles where agents in headsets, often standing and moving in a small square in front of their desks, could be seen making sales calls to their customers across the oceans. We could see tens of motivational banners vertically hanging from the ceiling, encouraging us to adopt traits that were conducive to global communication. For instance, motivational slogans about individual self ("believe in yourself") or time ("Make use of time, let not advantage slip")* were attempts to inspire new, globally compatible, habits of the mind that were slow to take hold among the agents who sang in groups with no concern about time as a resource to be exploited.

One of the advantages of doing participant observation is that one can feel what the others around are feeling. The researcher doesn't remain separate and above the population of study. I was awestruck by the feel of the floor, where the talk—what we could say, even after weeks of training, only haltingly—flowed freely from self-assured agents who were busy pitching sales to cultural others. We listened carefully as we barged in on calls, wonderstruck, hearing seasoned agents make an argument, convincing their customers for the telemarketing product. I was extremely nervous making my first live call from that room, as each of us was asked to make a real sales call, a call that didn't last for more than a minute; none of us trainees could

---

*Phrases used here are approximations of actual banner contents, which are avoided to protect GoCom's real identity.

generate a sale but Vikas and two others with prior call center experience were able to get a more patient hearing from their potential customers than the rest of us. When I barged in on calls, though, I also heard agents and customers talking past each other. Having lived in both the east and the west for long periods of my life, I could hear noncommunication between the two worlds. With no common experiences, values, and norms that could connect the agent and the customer, the bigger puzzle for me was: how could cultures talk at all at such a distance? Chapter 3 is a long and fairly involved answer to this puzzle.

## Neutral Accent

GoCom agents made calls to places they could not visit; they talked with people they would never meet. Oceans apart from those they served, they discussed with their customers intimate details of their lives, their plans, investments, purchases, and debts. Far apart yet so close. How could cultures talk in real time at such a distance unaided by the shared cultural, legal, or organizational symbolism? Even without physical distance, haven't we felt lost in foreign lands, missing—more often than not—cultural references used frequently? In the early 1990s when I arrived as a graduate student in California, I considered myself well prepared. I knew English relatively well, but I frequently missed my bus stops, failing to follow the driver's accent, and once embarrassed myself unwittingly by asking for a rubber from a female graduate student when I wanted to borrow an eraser,* and had no idea what *duh* meant even two years into the American culture. The lack of shared norms and values is often experienced as "culture shock" or

---

*In British English, "rubber" is often used to denote an eraser, whereas in American English it may refer, colloquially, to a condom.

what Bourdieu (1984) calls "hysteresis effect" when socialized expectations are not met. While physical proximity allows for a certain harmonization of expectations to emerge in regular settings, India's call center agents and their western clients did not enjoy such proximity.

Yet, in Gurgaon I saw agents pitching mortgages to Americans without ever visiting the United States, selling mobile connections to Londoners, and collecting debt from families in Florida. How did they wade through *double contingency*, a problem that plagues all communication? Double contingency, to put it simply, means that in order to speak I must already anticipate your expectations about what I want to say; your expectations that I can only imagine, and never really know, change what I say, and vice versa. For symbolic communication to succeed, George Herbert Mead (1922, 160) argued, one must assume the attitude of the other person and respond to it oneself. In the process, one ends up making one's speech contingent on the other's perspective, and vice versa (Schutz 1973). Following Mead, Talcott Parsons (1968) labeled it double contingency: John's action is contingent on not only Jean's probable overt reaction to his action, but also on what John interprets to be Jean's expectations about his behavior. And, ". . . this orientation to the expectation of the other is reciprocal or complementary" (Parsons and Shils, 1951, 105). Parsons thought that such complementarity was possible only because a pre-existing common culture assured that "actions, gestures, or symbols have more or less the same meaning for both ego and alter" (Parsons and Shils, 1951, 105). Instead of resolving double contingency, however, Parsons only managed to sweep it into the past, into an already-existing value consensus, which was assumed as the ever-present ground of all communication. It is not surprising that Parsons's solution fails to explain communication across continents with few common values, norms, expectations, and no visual cues or body language to facilitate conversations between Indian call center agents and their clients and customers in the United States, Britain, Australia, and Canada.

It took me a while to solve the riddle of communication. Only after going through the training at GoCom did I realize that call centers relied on the transmutation of cultural communication into global communication to facilitate these long-distance conversations. Two processes—neutralization and mimesis—were crucial to this transmutation. By *neutralization* I mean attempts at pruning unwanted cultural particulars while *mimesis* refers to simulating desired cultural elements.

Before I further discuss neutralization and mimesis and show how communication is facilitated through the neutralization of differences as well as the mimetic adoption of certain characteristics, let us be clear why global communication cannot utilize the working assumption of a common field of communication. The proliferation of global call centers elicits the question why it is not feasible to facilitate communication through usual interaction mechanisms.

## Global Talk

To my mind there are three kinds of distances that make call center communication a difficult enterprise: physical, cultural, and organizational. Physical distance makes communication a difficult endeavor even within a shared cultural framework. It is not surprising that the basic assumption of most social theories of communication is physical proximity. Physical metaphors abound in theories of symbolic interaction: the looking-glass self (Cooley 1902), front and back stage performances, face work, interaction rituals of casino gambling (Goffman 1959, 1967), dog fight and boxing (Mead 1934). Clearly, the sociology of communication has long assumed propinquity as the basis for interaction, gaining theoretical depth by analyzing face-to-face interaction.

Given the rise of virtual and online communities, one can criticize the "bias" toward face-to-face interaction as based in pretechnological assumptions of communicative possibility. But we must exercise caution in such criticisms because the emphasis on face-to-face interaction is often derived from perspectives of early socialization and childhood development for which physical interaction will always be of value. In step with theories of embodied cognition (Huttenlocher 2002; Lakoff and Johnson 1999; Lakoff and Núñez 2000), human and nonhuman animal studies show how brain areas involved in physical movement and cognitive learning are intimately connected, and physical activity is crucial to enhancing those neural connections (Hillman, Erickson, and Kramer 2008; Pellegrini and Smith 1998; Shephard et al. 1994); similarly, adverse effects of sedentary engagement with media screens on child development are well acknowledged (AAP 2011; Bar-on 2000). Everyday life experiences also suggest that the shaping of the self in infancy and early childhood takes place through physical interactions with parents. Clearly, the value of physical interaction in children's development is all the more important in a hypernetworked world of interaction (AAP 2011). Even for adults, persistent mobile communication is significantly linked to increased distress and decreased family satisfaction (Chesley 2005).

Yet, it is indubitable that virtual worlds and virtual social networks have thrived since the 1990s (Boellstorff 2008; Wellman 1999). Scholars have begun to formulate appropriate terminology for the virtual sphere reflected in distinctions, for instance, between embodied presence and response presence (Knorr Cetina and Bruegger 2002); while embodied presence is face-to-face, response presence allows responses to common objects without physical copresence. Yet, the success of response presence in online communities—from the early days of the WELL (Turner 2006) and Lambda-MOO (Turkle 1995)—has depended on a shared cultural framework and often a common purpose in interaction, allowing actors to operate within normal uncertainties of double contingency.

What compounds the problem of cultural distance is the issue of organizational distance between contracting companies, for instance, between Datys and Citibank. It has long been recognized that organizational culture inhabits and circulates through stories, myths, and symbols (Pettigrew 1979; Smircich 1983), giving organizations the status of speech communities (Barley 1983). The lack of a shared system of meaning or even a shared set of rules among global firms makes it difficult to take organizational communication among them for granted. Global outsourcing partners have increasingly found it difficult to forge a cultural unity even among subsidiaries of a putative single organization, let alone third parties. My participant observations at GoCom revealed that its organizational culture was quite different from that of American corporations. For instance, despite flattened hierarchies in India's call centers, the respect accorded to team leaders was far in excess of their actual status. The reason for this respect was partly due to the respect for age in Indian culture, and team leaders, in their thirties, were frequently older than agents, who were mostly in their twenties. Agents never called team leaders without adding "sir" or "madam" in every sentence. The language of hierarchy with Western customers was also audible in every conversation. Despite the trainer's warning, the trainees kept using "sir" in every sentence to address the mock customer, and later the actual customer. The use of "sir" in India derives from formal or age-based hierarchy that tends to clash with liberal individualism in the West. It was clear that agents' cultural habits were in conflict with the emerging evaluative scale of global communication, producing what Stark (2009) has called a sense of dissonance for participants.

Without physical proximity, or the working assumption of intersubjective concord through shared norms, rules, and cultural values or shared organizational meanings, the riddle of double contingency—how call center communication is possible at all—must be resolved through closer scrutiny of the space of communication. I start by positing a simple premise: to realize any corporate project of global communication, a certain leveling—the neutralization of difference—must be designed into the process. Here one detects the first feature of such projects: cultural neutralization, a mechanism that does not pretend to provide all the benefits of culturally dense conversations but a mechanism that reduces cultural specificity just enough for global communication to emerge. In actual fact, processes of cultural neutralization have limited success in transforming culturally mediated processes into global processes. Cultural particularities of speech, language, accent, values, norms remain important, even if they are disembedded from social aims of reaching understanding, acquiring an instrumental character oriented toward economic transactions in "market society" (Slater and Tonkiss 2001).

## Neutralization

In the 1990s, voice and accent training programs in India's call centers were geared toward imitation, i.e., training agents in India to mimic an American or a British accent. But poor imitation created more problems than it solved. A single mistake in recognizing the other person's accent or mispronouncing a common word meant sounding fake and losing the customer's trust. To add to the problem of trust, an agent trained in a single accent—British, American, Australian, or Canadian—would be locked into a process dedicated exclusively to one country, and managers would forfeit the ability to move the agent around in times of need.

The shift in approach required that the effort be directed at making communication possible instead of imitating accents. To understand and be understood by the other party, the pace, emphasis, intonation, and neutralization of the thickness of regional accents became more important than sounding like an American. Voice and accent trainers in most of the call centers switched to what they called accent neutralization, emphasizing the neutralization of regional accents in English, and reflecting a recalibration of sociocultural particularity to systemic requirements of the market society.

In personal interactions, agents and trainers frequently brought up the term *neutral accent*. My interview at Datys with Payal, as mentioned in the prologue, was the first instance that alerted me to the phenomenon of neutral accent (see Rivas [2007] and Rivero [2011] for similar uses of neutral Spanish and the locality of the translocal). To overcome regional and cultural marks, or communicative speed bumps, agents trained in what was termed a neutral accent or global accent, an accent more conducive to long-distance communication across cultures.

A crucial part of accent neutralization was the importance placed on the emphasis, or lexical stress. Geeta was unaware, prior to her training, of the fact of a predetermined emphasis on one or two syllables in all English words. Indeed, the notion of syllable, she mentioned, was new to her, prompting her to take detailed notes during training. Coming from a middle-class background, Geeta along with some of her peers seemed comfortable conversing in English, but faced with the trainer's push for including emphasis or stress in their accents, agents often appeared embarrassed, for instance, about not knowing that in *magnificent* the middle syllable is emphasized, not the first or last. Geeta mentioned that the name *Indianapolis* was particularly intriguing, as her native Hindi made it harder to put the emphasis on a syllable just before *polis*.

In a way, the adoption of emphasis in speech is simultaneously neutralizing and mimetic. While it tends to neutralize strong regional language influences within India, it also tends to mimic a general feature—lexical stress— in British, American, Australian, and Canadian accents (though the stress does not always fall on the same syllable in British and American English; e.g., see laboratory in British English, ləˈbɒr.ə.tri, versus American English, ˈlæb.rə.tɔˈr.i).

Accent neutralization has evolved into a business of its own. Kiran Aggarwal, the chief executive of DialAct, a firm that trained call center agents in matters of language and accent, revealed in an interview that accent neutralization was now a global business. Ms. Aggarwal, an energetic but soft-spoken woman in her late thirties, discussed how her firm was engaged in projects with a number of call centers in Mumbai (India), Manila (Philippines), and Kuala Lumpur (Malaysia). A global endeavor, accent neutralization was a technical solution to the problem of real-time communication across cultures. The solution was technical not only in the sense of techniques of accent neutralization; it was also technical because it arose, not out of social needs for cross-cultural understanding but out of demands for an uninterrupted flow of services through a global hierarchy of labor (Mirchandani 2005; Poster and Wilson 2008). It reproduced in culturally specific forms a labor process that had earlier proved onerous in advanced economies (Taylor and Bain 2005). Agents invented their own mnemonic techniques to remember the emphasis on different syllables. As her notes show, Geeta started capitalizing the syllables that needed emphasis in speech as shown in figure 3.1.

Often, agents rewrote English words in Hindi, a common yet curious practice because English and Hindi languages share few sounds for vowels or consonants. Yet the reason was easy to decipher. Hindi uses a highly phonetic script, Devnagari, which makes it easier to memorize the pronunciation of certain English words in Hindi that are traditionally pronounced incorrectly, or too differently in Indian English. While all agents were comfortable reading and writing in English, they resorted to the Hindi script, ironically, to avoid slipping back into regional accents; neutral accent was supposed to emerge after practicing stress, pace, and diction for a few months.

The construction of neutral accent was thus performative in J. L. Austin's (1962) sense. Austin argued against a positivist claim that our utterances always describe something and, therefore, must either be true or false. Utterances, as illocutionary acts, can also perform an action (e.g., a priest declaring someone a husband or wife at a wedding ceremony). Thus, if call centers establish a certain pronunciation as neutral, it does, for the future, become neutral, at least in the context of global communication initiated by call centers.

A neutral accent may come to denote a placeless variation of an accent. Consider the pronunciation of *laboratory*; we note that both British and American versions drop an "o," the former being *laboratry* (lə'bɒr.ə.tri) and the latter *labratory* ('læb.rə.tɔːr.i). We can imagine a placeless alternative that drops neither. Although the development of neutral accent may not be as systematic, one can see how possibilities are being explored in India's call centers through conscious efforts at deregionalizing and removing place marks from an accent, thus making it unmarked. True, in order to know what is unmarked, we need to make all the accents available, something impossible, but Indian call centers are aware of a large set of regional Indian accents, and they try to neutralize the information brought out by such regional accents so that it sounds placeless to them. If call centers succeed in performing a neutral accent that allows a certain placelessness to emerge, it does become neutral in that regard.

Despite the reasonable success of training in accent neutralization, however, agents found it difficult to change or neutralize their accents. As embodied forms of culture, accents are difficult to relinquish or acquire in a short period (Bourdieu 1986). It takes time and a younger mind. Despite

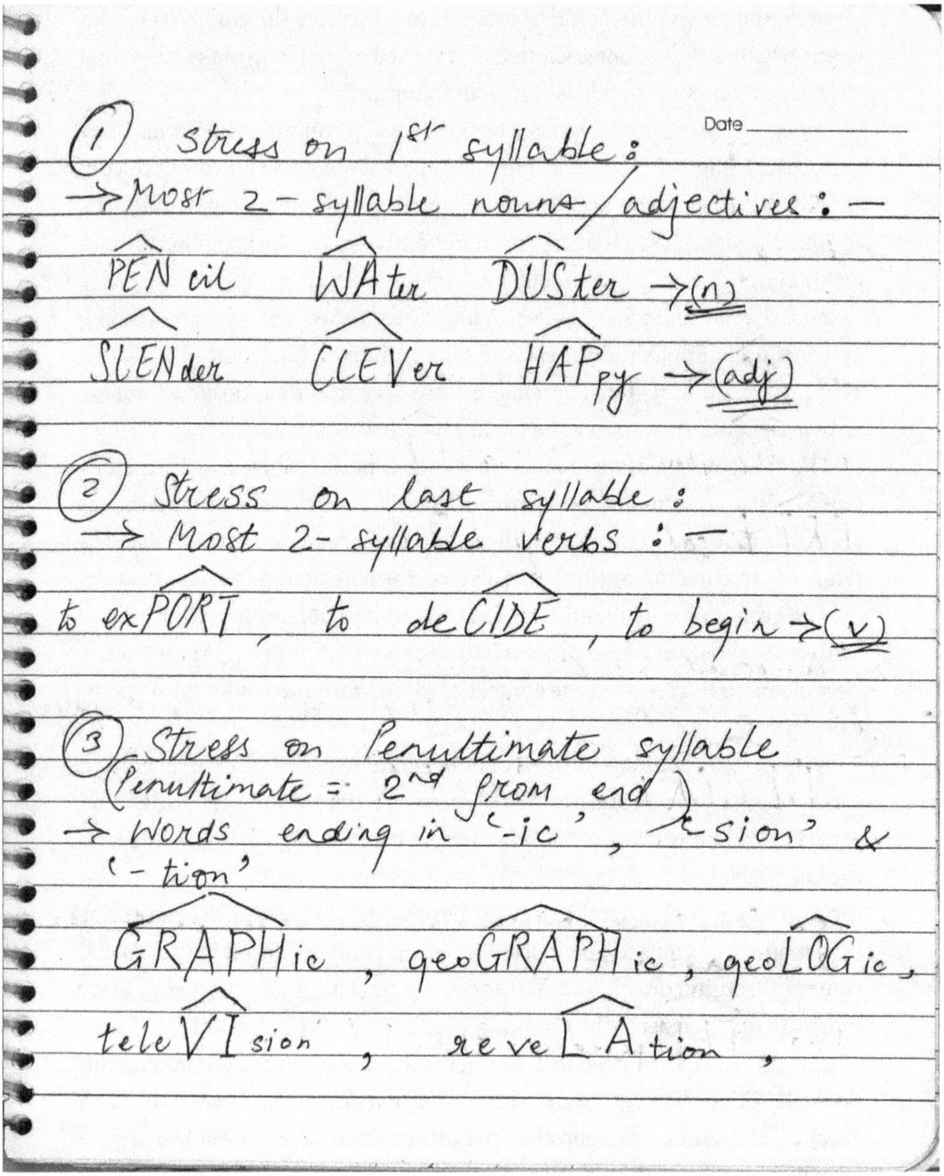

① Stress on 1st syllable:

→ Most 2-syllable nouns/adjectives: —

PEN cil    WAter    DUSter → (n)

SLENder    CLEVer    HAPpy → (adj)

② Stress on last syllable:
→ Most 2-syllable verbs : —

to exPORT , to deCIDE , to begin → (v)

③ Stress on Penultimate syllable
(Penultimate = 2nd from end)
→ Words ending in '-ic', '-sion' &
'-tion'

GRAPHic , geoGRAPHic , geoLOGic ,

teleVIsion , reveLAtion ,

FIGURE 3.1. Stressed syllables

long training sessions, one could witness how accents were after all seamless expressions of the body, linking movements of the tongue, teeth, larynx, and neural wiring. Recent brain imaging results suggest that languages literally tune the cortex (Tan et al. 2003), making it harder to learn the second language later in life (Huttenlocher 2002; Marian et al. 2003). And surprisingly, learning a second language also changes the functional brain network of the first language (Zou et al. 2012). In the case of language, the social seems to affect the biological, and vice versa.

Most agents attempted, often unsuccessfully, to imitate the neutral accent of their team leader, who was also Indian, just a little more experienced. Tarun admitted: "You tend to ape him [team leader], you tend to do the way he talks, the way he speaks, but he's got a lot more experience than what you have; so you may pick up a few lines from whatever he converses but it may not add up to entire communication." It was not easy to turn a culturally sculpted identity into a globally neutral one. Failures of accent neutralization were often audible as I barged in on calls on the floor when the agent and the customer could not fully understand each other. Later it became clearer when my research assistant, an American graduate student, tried to transcribe my tape-recorded interviews with Indian agents, and had a difficult time understanding their putative neutral accents.

Clearly, accent neutralization programs enjoyed only partial success in neutralizing the influence of regional languages. Here the relationship between neutralization and mimesis becomes visible: the partial neutralization of regional accents was conducted through mimetic selections from certain features of British and American accents, which often acquired a placeless character partly because agents could not fully imitate them. Mimesis and neutralization thus emerged as particular forms of selection and deselection that made global communication possible. The mimesis part of the process, though existent, was not clear to agents who often did not know if theirs was a British or American variation. As I mentioned earlier, the pronunciation of *laboratory*, written in Hindi script by Geeta in figure 3.2 below, was actually its British version, but clearly, she was not aware of its Britishness because she marked it as "global accent" after being so informed by her trainer. *Global accent* was often used interchangeably with *neutral accent* by trainers and agents alike.

The term *neutral* is therefore a strategic construction in global communication, and its meaning keeps changing depending on slight variations in the trainer's background. For example, Cowie (2007) found that older staff

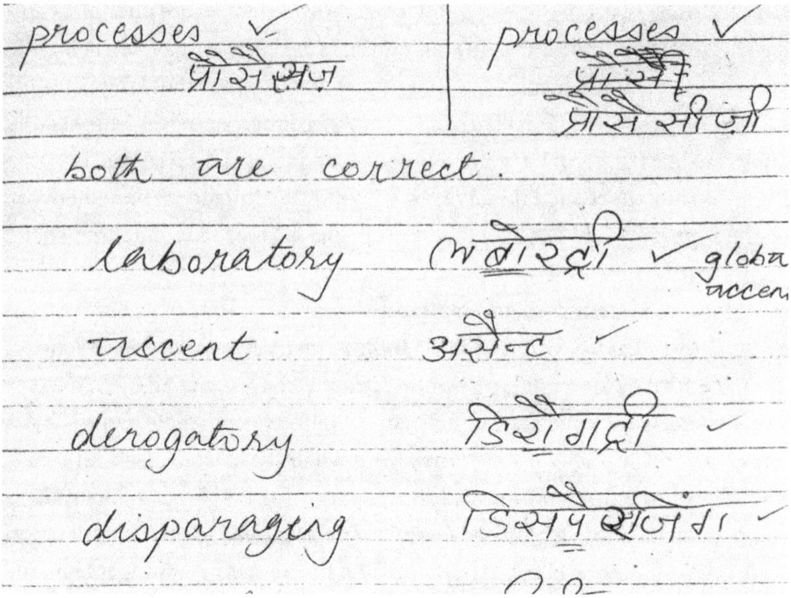

FIGURE 3.2. English in Hindi

members, who might see their role as one promoting a shift in the direction of "educated Indian English," emphasized its British origins while younger staff members shifted toward American accents. One may debate whether this training constitutes accent neutralization, but the reason call centers termed it *neutralization* is due perhaps to their focus on certain key features of English speech that persist, to a degree, in all dominant accents: British, American, Canadian, and Australian. By focusing attention on these common features, the trainer is able to mitigate, not eliminate, the effects of local and regional influences on the agent's speech. Neutralization allows, only to a degree, the unhinging of speech from its cultural moorings and links it with purposes of global business.

During training, the transmutation of cultural into global processes reached beyond accents, affecting everyday cultural understanding and modes of conversation. Agents needed to take account of their cultural, often unconscious, habits of conversation, and learn a different style of interaction. They were asked to act according to an evaluative scale (Stark 2009) different from what guided their culturally specific ways of speaking, including gender and age-based socialization in humility and hierarchy.

Their behavioral training emphasized "polite assertiveness" while adopting a neutral stance toward gender or age of their American customers.

For instance, Goswami continuously received remarks about being "too polite." He was working for the debt collection process and received the following note from his team leader: "Assume. Don't ask. Need to take control of the talk. Just ask who you are talking to, then start asking the first name of the person." This style of speech with its undertones of individual autonomy and equality was something alien to call center employees, something different from their cultural upbringing in north India where one respected the elderly and advised the young. The difference between two sets of socialization—social identity derived from primary socialization and system identity attained through attempts at cultural neutralization—led to what Costello (2005) has appropriately termed *identity dissonance*, marking a clash between the habitus and the field of global business communication (see also Stark [2009]). Here I agree with Xiang Biao (2007) that it is not enough to explore the social embeddedness of markets; it is equally important to understand its obverse: the transformation of the social by market imperatives.

In this new identity, relatively neutral to their sociocultural world, agents sought to adapt to a way of speech that was more common, for instance, in the telemarketing culture largely invented in the United States. While some of this knowledge and training is generic to telemarketing or call center industry worldwide, its basic ingredients derived from social norms and values of North American culture that were still foreign in India. It is not surprising that India's call centers, despite relying on a more educated and full-time workforce, have work systems that are more tightly constrained, monitored, and standardized than those found among U.S. subcontractors, as identified by Batt, Doellgast, and Kwon (2005), who also report that supervisors provide feedback and coaching on a weekly or daily basis in 94 percent of the offshore centers but in only 46 and 55 percent of the U.S. in-house and outsourced centers. This reflects the importance of coaching for Indian agents, whose work has the added dimension of culture work.

It would be inaccurate to consider the processes of neutralization as unique to global call centers or to define global communication in opposition to local or national communication just as it would be a mistake to define the global itself—whether an institution, a process, or a discursive practice—in opposition to national states, for the global may reside in national territories and transform national processes from within (Sassen 2007). In many ways, immigrant language training programs as well as diversity training programs in American workplaces are global processes taking place in national territories negotiating the problem of cross-cultural communication.

Notions of neutralization and mimesis are portable to work settings that require training in intercultural communication for an increasingly diverse workforce in presumably local corporations. Yet there is also a crucial difference: immigrants' physical presence and their long-term objectives in settling down in a new society differentiate them from call center agents, underscoring a different relationship with the culture of interest. No call center agent at GoCom, my field research revealed, had ever visited the United States in person.

But neutralization addresses only one side of transmutation: it weeds out elements that are not functional in the new system. It is an important but not sufficient condition for the possibility of global communication. Differences in accents or the complex cultural grammar of age hierarchy do not serve an immediate function in global business communication; often, they obstruct clear understanding. Neutralization is a process through which less functional elements of culture are rendered ineffective. Does this point to a complete standardization or bureaucratization of communication? Indeed not. Here, the second feature of transmutation—mimesis—reflects a process of selecting and absorbing rather than that of discarding. Instead of neutralizing or reducing cultural particularities, mimesis refers to attempts at simulating cultural lifeworlds that are functional for global business. In fact, such nonstandardized elements of communication as cheerfulness, enthusiasm, and empathy are encouraged and augmented, through mimesis, to achieve predictable outcomes even while the process of neutralization discourages and makes ineffective the elements out of step with global demands. Here one's respect for older persons may be reconfigured to function as politeness toward the customer in a hierarchical order, transmuting a cultural trait into a more useful "the-customer-is-king" orientation.

## Mimesis

For global communication to take place, therefore, the neutralization of cultural difference is not sufficient; it is equally important for a complementary process to happen as well. Economic function must be dressed up, for instance, in culturally approved expressions for the communication to succeed. Vikas once worked at a call center that used a performance evaluation chart where three out of six variables pertained to such expressions, namely, "Be polite and friendly," "Demonstrate emotions," and "Tone/Attitude," in addition to such information-seeking variables as "Solicit information about the debtor" or "Thinking ahead and counter questioning" or "Ask assumptive questions." Most of the motivational banners hanging from the ceiling at GoCom also encouraged traits that were conducive to global business communication.

The use of appropriate expressions while communicating with another culture was an important aspect of both telemarketing and debt collection calls. It was clearly visible in cases where agents were trained how to react to negative responses from consumers; what kind of readymade phrases or common rebuttals, wrapped up in an appropriate tone, they could employ to keep the conversation going, and avert the premature end of the call by the customer. They had to acquire the habit of feeling sorry, for instance, for someone whose spouse had met with an accident but without losing the track of where the conversation was supposed to go. The agents, as shown in Geeta's handwritten notes in figure 3.3, were asked to learn and come up with appropriate responses for particular situations.

Some of this work falls within the scope of emotional labor. We have learned from Arlie Hochschild (1983) about the trained management of emotions in businesses—airlines to restaurants—and the work that goes into exhorting appropriate feelings. While the agents' work was never too far from emotional labor, their major effort lay in pursuing a different cultural logic. We may complement "emotion work" with "culture work" in our case. The meaning of some cultural expressions was not native to the agents' culture. American flight attendants, Hochschild's focus, performed emotional expressions that were, at least, American in shape and form. Indian call center agents performed, in their second language, expressions that often didn't ring a bell for them. Frequently, they needed to weave mimetically an unfamiliar cultural logic into their conversational strategy.

However, emotional performance was equally important. The performance of an upbeat mood was a requirement. Radha, another agent, who sounded formal and strained on the phone, was advised to keep a smiling face while talking with her overseas clients. When she objected that her clients could not possibly see her face on the phone, she was quickly corrected with general advice that friendly voices can only proceed from friendly faces. Smiles did convert into talk. There were remarks to this effect on her performance evaluations.

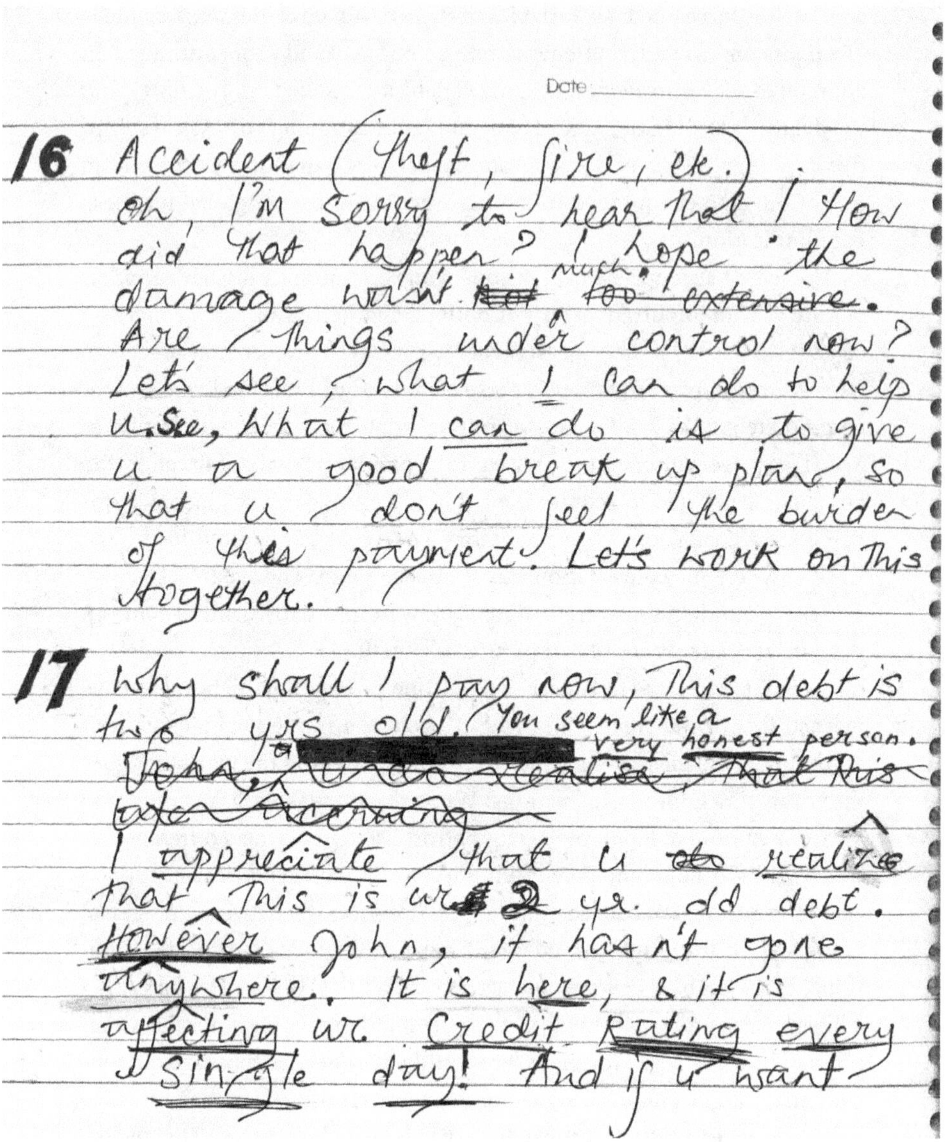

**16** Accident (theft, fire, etc.)
Oh, I'm sorry to hear that! How did that happen? I hope the damage wasn't ~~too~~ much extensive. Are things under control now? Let's see, what I can do to help u. See, what I can do is to give u a good break up plan, so that u don't feel the burden of this payment! Let's work on this together.

**17** Why shall I pay now, this debt is two yrs old. You seem like a very honest person. ~~John, u do realise that this extra accruing~~ I appreciate that u ~~do~~ realize that this is ur 2 yr. old debt. However John, if hasn't gone anywhere. It is here, & it is affecting ur Credit Rating every single day! And if u want

FIGURE 3.3. Emotion-culture work

"Sometimes they yell: smile! You're not smiling." Sanjay corroborated Radha's statement, "They say when you smile, they [customers] also smile on the phone."

Putting on a smile for a stranger, let us note, has never been part of India's public culture or business culture. While in the United States, it is quite common for strangers on the street, especially sidewalks, to make eye contact, say "hi," nod, or smile at each other, in India there are no comparable public norms of attention. On the other hand, once an acquaintance has been made, Indian culture allows for quicker friendships and less guarded privacy. Radha's lack of smile in a phone conversation with a stranger was a culturally typical trait, particularly for women in the gendered context of north India, that needed to be transformed, through mimesis, to be part of a globally spreading business culture. In line with the thesis of emotional labor (Hochschild 1983), here one can see how human affects have been incorporated into capital, and how the affective labor of contact and interaction further creates and manipulates affects like the feeling of ease and well-being (Hardt 1999).

Like neutralization, mimesis helped to produce a common ground for global communication. While less functional elements like regional accents were handed over to neutralization processes, useful traits were adapted for the new system of communication through mimetic processes. Agents were given common names from the culture of interest, reflecting what Winifred Poster (2007) has termed "national identity management." So, Vikas served as Victor while Radha became Ruth in a world where their identities mimicked generalized identities of cultures they were serving. It built credibility and trust in matters of debt, default, and general finance where shame and suspicion often shaped conversations. Clearly, global communication made national identity conspicuous, and the call center management worked hard to mask the national origin of its employees (Poster 2007) even at the risk of losing employee loyalty (Das, Dharwadkar, and Brandes 2008).

"Some call centers call them only by their alias name," Tarun said light-heartedly, "so some people also suffer from identity crisis." When I asked him if he ever made a mistake telling his real name to a customer, he explained it was the other way round: "No, even sometimes I get a call at home . . . Who is this? This is Tim. It happens by mistake because, because 300 times you have said, my name is Tim, hi this is Tim calling."

I have explored briefly the notion of mimicry in the context of India's call centers in my previous work (Aneesh 2006, 2007), and many others have done it at length, particularly the adoption of foreign accents, identities, lifestyles, and customs (Mirchandani 2012; Nadeem 2011; Poster 2007). Its comic version has touched the American popular culture through documentaries as well as a film and TV show, viz., *Outsourced*.

While in agreement with accounts of mimicry, I want to shift the emphasis from copying to recoding: instead of simply copying, mimesis recodes cultural expressions with noncultural functions without making it apparent, triggering a transmutation that allows global business communication to appear as everyday cultural communication. Mimetic training was not confined to the acquisition of new names. It also required cultural expressions to go with them.

"We get a list of American terms, especially related to the process," Geeta recalled. "The terms and words that you will come across frequently. So that's why you have this one and a half to two months of training, which deals with every aspect of that call." Long sessions were devoted to learning American or British informal expressions through formal training. Although the language of communication was English, it was not certain if most agents understood such common informal expressions as "dude," "jerk," or "nuts." Geeta took copious notes in class, learning, for instance, that a "geek" is "someone who works too hard, is more intelligent than usual, & is slightly unattractive." They had not grown up hearing these expressions in India. Excerpts from Geeta's notebook, as shown in figure 3.4, support the assertion that global business communication is made possible by training agents in minute details of the client's culture, requiring them to memorize ordinary colloquial terms with which they may not be familiar.

Understanding cultural expressions without their repeated everyday context is an improbable endeavor. Many call centers showed films, which to a degree helped with both the accent and cultural context of particular terms and styles of speech. Agents were encouraged to watch specific films on their own.

"I go to the library and watch Oscar-winning movies," Sanjay mentioned.

"Do you remember the movies they show you?" I couldn't stop my curiosity.

"Yeah. *My Fair Lady*, I remember," Sanjay recalled. Quite odd, I thought, for it was a rather old and very British film based on Bernard Shaw's play; Sanjay said that they watched it to familiarize themselves with the British accent.

"For the U.S.," Sanjay reported, "they showed us *Friends*, the TV show."

Despite mimetic training in everyday culture, it would be a mistake to think that its goal was to become indistinguishable from quotidian forms of cultural conversation, a fact that became obvious when some Americans, in calmer

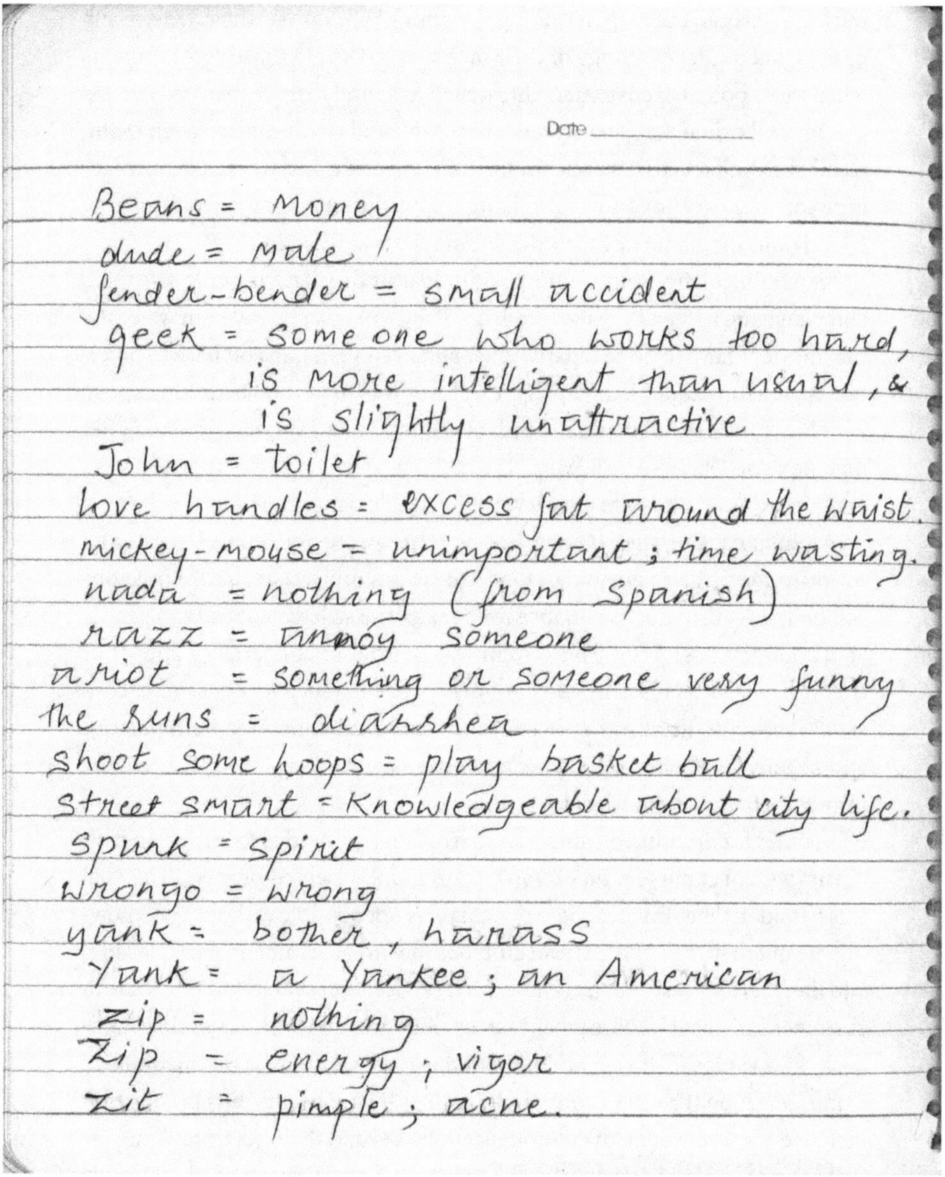

Beans = money
dude = male
fender-bender = small accident
geek = some one who works too hard,
        is more intelligent than usual, &
        is slightly unattractive
John = toilet
love handles = excess fat around the waist.
mickey-mouse = unimportant; time wasting.
nada = nothing (from Spanish)
razz = annoy someone
a riot = something or someone very funny
the runs = diarrhea
shoot some hoops = play basketball
street smart = knowledgeable about city life.
spunk = spirit
wrongo = wrong
yank = bother, harass
Yank = a Yankee; an American
zip = nothing
Zip = energy; vigor
zit = pimple; acne.

FIGURE 3.4. Formal training in informal expressions

moments, would open up, narrating their entire life stories, their dreams and desires, and understandings of their own world. During those very moments when these potential customers threatened to sound real, they wasted agents' precious talk-time. Ranjana, a student at Jawaharlal Nehru University in Delhi, recalled a similar experience at a call center where she had worked the preceding year. She was not allowed to hang up on the customer even if it meant losing time and financial incentives for other possible sales.

"Sometimes, they start chatting with you as if they have nothing else to do and you made a free call," she recalled. "They will talk and say I am watching this movie, I have to go to a party, what should I wear, and you have to entertain them. You cannot hang up. So, there was this man I spoke to . . . I spoke with him for three hours, three hours straight, in one of my sittings, and after that, he said, 'Oh, my wife is back.' I said, 'Wow!' He said, 'I was getting bored, I do not work. It's my wife who is working, and I just get bored at home.'"

As Ranjana, Goswami, Geeta, and all others were not allowed to hang up on customers, their half-understood life stories only wasted those precious call hours. A customer's relevance for her job was strictly reduced to a profile as a potential customer. The system was neutral to concerns of agents or customers even as it attempted a mimesis of social life. Yet occasional conversations with flirtatious or humorous customers contained both positive and negative elements, reflecting, as Noronha and D'Cruz (2007) argue, the inherent duality of experience.

In order for the mimetic processes to work, agents needed to learn who their clients were. Let me give an example from a U.S.-oriented process. The goal was to understand American identity; this was not possible without also knowing the micro details of American attitudes toward government, work, leisure, and life. Previous research has shown that service representatives contribute to customer satisfaction more when they exhibit the characteristics of thoroughness, knowledgeableness, and preparedness, regardless of the medium of communication (Froehle 2006). In the case of Indian agents, this preparation included the knowledge of cultural locations beyond their horizon. Being far away, the new culture and upbringing was available to these agents, not directly but through scripts they read and memorized, as shown in figure 3.5.

The awareness, "There is dignity of labour in their country," is poignant, given that these workers tended to have uncertain dignity in their mimetic renderings of global communication. Despite extraordinary efforts at cultural mimesis, contingencies continued to haunt global communication.

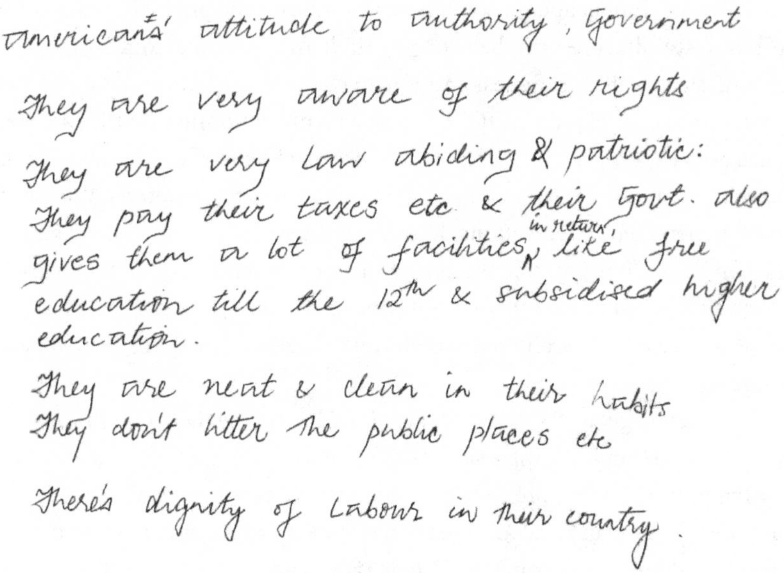

Americans' attitude to Authority, Government

They are very aware of their rights

They are very law abiding & patriotic:
They pay their taxes etc & their Govt. also
gives them a lot of facilities, in return, like free
education till the 12th & subsidised higher
education.

They are neat & clean in their habits
They don't litter the public places etc

There's dignity of labour in their country.

FIGURE 3.5. American attitudes

"The moment they start talking about baseball, you have absolutely no idea what's going on there. And they start asking, do you have the tickets?" Tarun explained his frustration about not knowing much about baseball living in a country crazy about cricket, and joked, "And I say, yes, we have the tickets, dammit, do you have a house, can you tell me? Is it a condominium?" Tarun sold mortgages for the client of his call center.

"Just because [a service] has been outsourced," Tarun complained, "companies think, they are going to get the same level of services . . . but they have to understand the constraints. The premise is that within a three-week [period] of time you have to have a grasp of the culture, the language, the process." He highlighted the importance of the cultural context of speech, "Most of the people, like I, come from a very small town, I come from Patna, you must have heard of it . . . You don't spend more than three or four minutes a day on the phone, and here you are maxed out at something like seven and a half hours. And you are talking about things that you have absolutely no idea about. I have never seen a condo or cabins, studios and cabins," for which he was selling mortgages.

In reality, Indian agents could never be rude on the phone but they were often destabilized by the behavior of their American customers in their openness as well as rudeness. American customers at times conveyed nationalistic or racial judgment. Just as visual cultures of race on the Internet have been explored by Lisa Nakamura (2008), scholars of call centers, Kiran Mirchandani (2012), for instance, have begun to analyze aural cultures of race. In personal conversations, however, I did not hear complaints against racism per se. It is possible the agents misrecognized racism as "rudeness" when they heard it. And there was a consensus among them that American customers were generally ruder than Australian, Canadian, or British customers.

"When you get to know your callers [and hear] how they react to you . . . [it's disheartening]," Sanjay said. "Americans are very rude . . . You know I was thinking that they are rude to us because we call them again and again, but they are rude in general." He recalled talking to an Indian woman who had moved to Mexico from the United States, and she told him, "Compared to when I lived in America, I'm far better off in Mexico . . . I don't know Spanish, so I only speak with those Mexicans who speak English."

"[British] are very decent," Sanjay ruminated. "They are always known for this thing. And they hardly cuss at you, cuss you and abuse you. . . . In a month, probably a single person. And in America two or three people in a day . . . You will get two or three people who are rude." But Sanjay also admitted that the British may have been nice on the phone but they were hard to convince: "And in the UK it's very hard to crack the sale. You know, what I believe if you can crack the sale telemarketing in UK, then you can do it in any other country. Because it's as difficult as India."

Sanjay was not biased against his American customers in any way. The best story about Sanjay was told to me by his friend Tarun who worked in the same call center. Sanjay often answered his regular phone with his call center name, Sam. "Actually, he would say my name is Sam on the phone sometimes," Tarun remembered. "This is Sam, I am calling from Parsec Finances." With bermuda shorts and a ponytail, "he looks more American than any of you," Tarun joked.

"There was a mirror placed in front of our work stations," Tarun narrated, "because they found, you can imagine, that if you slouch, you can see yourself in the mirror and see that you're slouching." The mechanism was used for people to stop slouching and be attentive. This had a big effect on Sanjay's attitude as he extended the mirror's function to include his general behavior. "He started getting this notion that if you look like an American," Tarun continued, "you will talk like an American." Sanjay thought if he dressed like an American, and looked so in the mirror, he would talk and behave like an American. However, Sanjay's real-time interactions with Americans shattered some of his illusions.

"I chat with Americans or I go to a typical American chat room," Sanjay recalled, "[and I see] all the cussing, all the fighting, all that in the chat room . . . Probably they are frustrated and they take out their frustration on us . . . whatever it is . . . They're not polite." Sadder and wiser, Sanjay still decided to keep his bermuda shorts and ponytail.

While American openness with meandering personal stories hindered sales, their rudeness was a personal affront. From his experiences working for different call centers, Sanjay realized that he was made to intrude into the privacy of Americans during their evening meal hours or leisure time. What he did not know was the fact that the scripted version of Americans he came to know during his training left out, for obvious reasons, strict American notions of private and public time, notions that were not shared in the same way by British, Australian, or Indian forms of sociality. He could hear their anger at this invasion of privacy, and experienced culture shock without ever visiting the United States.

The illustrations above make it clear that a well-known global economic hierarchy is still at work. Neutralization and mimesis are at work only in one direction. There is no pressure, at least currently, on American or British cultures for communicative adaptation, as they are not required to simulate Indian cultural traits.

But notions of class and national hierarchies tell an incomplete story. We must also think of global communication as a system where *who* controls is a less important question than *how* it is controlled. American or British customers, while on the positive end of global hierarchy, appeared to be at the mercy of global communication systems in their own way. Individual identities and behaviors in the United States are increasingly simulated at the systemic level in numerous databases, covering one's credit scores, buying habits, demographic characteristics such as age, gender, income, race, region, and education. Thus, customers are transformed, often without their knowledge, into data profiles to meet certain conditions of communication. Indeed, most outbound global calls, pertaining to telemarketing or debt collection, were not initiated by agents in Gurgaon. They were initiated by a software program called Dialer that targeted specific profiles—demographic, economic, and cultural—of American and British clientele, increasing the chances of successful connections between the agents and their customers, a form of communication that was not started by either party, even though the two found themselves engaged in a real-time conversation.

It was not only Radha who found herself transformed into a form of data called Ruth whose previous "real" self was now a glitch to be trained and corrected, whose accented English needed to be neutralized in favor of the global English required for global communication. Her customers, too, were only particular profiles, neutralized and mimicked by the global system of communication.

In short, processes of neutralization and mimesis enable the formation of a global communication system by filtering and adopting elements crucial to its function. It is important to note that the two processes are not at odds with each other. They may often be present in the same act of speech or communication. In addition to my earlier example of bureaucratic transmutation, let us consider the example of cartography, which is not connected to the topic at hand and thus may shed light on how the theoretical relationship between neutralization and mimesis is conceptualized. A system of mapping neutralizes distance even as it produces a mimesis of territory through scaling and coding, resulting in the transmutation of real space. Mimesis is never simple copying or re-presentation. The transmutation achieved through neutralization and mimesis allows maps to generate features that eyes cannot often see in real space; e.g., maps of crime rates, poverty, income, education. The map transforms real space into something that is functional for different investigations and knowledge. The field of global business communication discussed here is not neutral, quite like the map, in its effects as it harbors specific goals and purposes; it seeks to neutralize only those cultural specificities that present obstacles in its operation. The problem occurs when its perspective is enforced as the sole perspective available, devaluing experiences arising from differences that fail to register as important for global concerns.

The second manner in which neutrality and mimesis come together pertains to the way scripts of neutralization spread around the world through mimetic diffusion. Using the world society perspective (Krücken and Drori 2009), one can foresee how scripts of neutrality may spread through cultural rationalization in a stateless and liberal world society (Lechner and Boli 2005; Meyer 2009; Meyer et al. 1997). In 2013, training programs for teaching assistants at a research university were found to be using "neutral accent" as the goal for foreign-born graduate students. Elements of accent

neutralization may be in the process of being adopted through simple mim-
icries of rational scripts.

For future research, notions of neutralization and mimesis suggest in-
quiring into emergent forms of communication where instead of socializing
agents into neutralized and mimetic speech, software programs are written
to perform a similar mimesis of requisite social communication. Attempts
at representing human speech through artificial intelligence have frequently
failed to meet expectations because human intelligence and machine intelligence process speech and information in drastically different ways (Dreyfus
1979). Yet, recent developments suggest that it is not the replication of
human intelligence but its functional mimesis—with all associated dangers
of machine-based decision-making (Dreyfus, Dreyfus, and Athanasiou
2000)—that is at work. To perform a mimesis of chess skills, for instance,
IBM's program Deep Blue, in a match against Garry Kasparov, did not employ human skills that include instant pattern recognition and immense intuition through a lifetime of experience. Indeed, intelligence of the machine
that evaluated 200 million positions per second was in total contrast with
those of Kasparov, who could evaluate only 2–6 positions per second. But
the program did produce a functional mimesis of human skills by challenging a highly skilled player. Recently, Microsoft research developed a medical
avatar project where a woman's face on a computer screen talks to patients,
understands their speech, recognizes their conditions, and reasons to make
an initial diagnosis of their ailment and its seriousness. The project leader
noted, "Our young children and grandchildren will think it is completely
natural to talk to machines that look at them and understand them" (Lohr
and Markoff 2010). Just as call center agents need not internalize cultural
frames and values of another culture and need only to be able to perform
sufficiently well to fulfill their function, it is likely that a great number of
social conversations in the future may be addressed not to trained agents but
to programmed avatar interfaces, a fact one already notices in its embryonic
form in everyday routine communication with computer-based systems
(e.g., calling banks, airlines, and other companies like Microsoft). It is important for sociological research to investigate such developments, even if,
or perhaps because, they are not really but only mimetically social in nature,
for they give us an inkling of the future of social communication.

While global businesses seem to depend on neutralization and mimesis
to develop the field of global communication, the problem of double contingency is never fully solved. The transmutation of cultural communication is

never complete, and the cultural seams of global talk tend to assert themselves frequently, highlighting the unresolved contingencies of communication. Contingencies often arose due to problems of human-machine interface. Global communication lacks the social context of speech. The only context available is the one provided by customer relations databases, which are integrated into the process of making calls through dialer software programs, targeting select database profiles.

## System Identities: *Divergent Itineraries and Uses of Personality*

April 2005. India's first call center fraud occupied the news headlines, sending nervous jitters through the young industry. Five employees at MphasiS, a call center in charge of Citibank operations, pulled off a financial fraud worth nearly half a million dollars. Coming from middle-class families, the accused employees—unit supervisor Maurelene Fernandes, Bijoy Alexander, and former call center agents Ivan Thomas, Siddhartha Mehta, and Stephan Daniel—had no previous criminal record. They did not break through the firewalls or hack the systems used by MphasiS. There was no breach or audit failure. These young employees were privy to account holders' information. The only pieces missing were the PINs, the keys to customers' financial identities, which the prime accused in the fraud obtained by "sweet-talking" five account holders.

"Once you give your house keys to the thief, there's bound to be havoc," Sanjay Jadhav, assistant commissioner of police, remarked on the theft, blaming the victims (Vaidya 2005). Once obtained, the PINs allowed the five young workers to free their customers' system identities from their social world to their own advantage. In the space of four months, nearly half a million dollars were withdrawn from their bank accounts and transferred to fictitious accounts opened in India.

Stolen identities! Just a few decades ago, it would be hard to explain what it means except in cases of impersonation. Even the media clamor in the United States about identity theft fails to capture how fundamentally social life has differentiated in multiple ways. The much-discussed information revolution, dating to the close of World War II, has actually changed certain important rules of social life. More than pleasing interconnections and efficient economies, the information age has reduced the reliance on the immediate world—our behavioral performances for relatives, neighbors, friends, and strangers—by adding something quite different: behavioral performances for abstract systems, including but not limited to the systems of credit rating, surveillance, retailing, biomedicine, and systems of examination. While stolen identities are only a small part of the picture, they do illuminate the existence and importance of system identity and how it affects people's credit scores and life chances.

Cases of identity theft are not unique to India's call centers. The rate of identity theft is much greater in the United States, partly because of the larger production of system identities. "I mean, your credit score is basically all you have," Andrew Sobanet says in a video on the Federal Trade Commission (FTC) website. In 2010, about 8.1 million Americans were reported to be victims of identity theft, representing only a fraction of the estimated victim population (Finklea 2012).

For India, no reliable comparable data are available, but an estimate from Gurgaon of forty identity theft cases in 2011 would perhaps make it less than a thousand cases for the country in 2010 (Dhankhar 2012). In the case of the United States, the question is how identity theft has come to be so routine in everyday life. The above case only highlights the distance from which system identities could be stolen with unsettling effects on people's putative real lives.

But let us not exaggerate the effects of identity theft; customers' losses are absorbed by retailers, banks, and credit card companies in most cases of theft. The problem of identity theft lies less in the domain of theft and more in the domain of identity restoration work that must follow afterward. In itself, identity theft is not as important as media reports often suggest, Cole and Pontell (2006) alert us, and the moral panic created by the reports can be used to increase the scale and scope of surveillance, increasing the amount of data collected on individuals. Indeed, the dynamic that is important is not identity theft but data collection, whose theft, misuse, and abuse can take disquieting forms. Cases of identity theft are interesting only in the way they underscore general developments.

In recent decades, modes of existence have multiplied, particularly in the United States. Apart from physical and virtual forms of togetherness (e.g., virtual communities on the web), one also exists in the form of data. One's credit history, buying habits, medical history, and demographics such as age, gender, region, and education all produce multiple constructions of personality—of which one is even not aware oneself. These "digital personae," to use Roger Clarke's (1994) phrase, have not only attained a degree of autonomy from the physical self, they have also become more effective in predicting one's life chances. For instance, in order to get a loan for purchasing a house in the United States, one's credit score—usually described through a FICO (Fair-Isaac Corporation) score—may be a better predictor of one's chances of getting a good annual percentage rate (APR) for the loan than one's cultural or social capital.

When I moved from California to Wisconsin, I knew few people besides my immediate family. My social network was limited to the peers who hired me for the new position. Being an immigrant, I lacked the savoir-faire of the native. How was I able to receive a large home loan at a good interest rate? The short answer: my FICO score, about which I was only dimly aware. For better or worse, one's extensive social network, one's attire, speech, and the polished sureness of social behavior are no longer enough to arouse trust in a banker. In order to impress a bank officer or a mortgage broker, one must now tweak one's FICO profile through techniques of improving credit history. One may want to lower debt, pay bills on schedule, and have a longer credit history for the system. One must not open or close too many credit card accounts too quickly or let frequent inquiries be made into one's credit history because the financial system registers this behavior as volatile.

Despite cases of racial profiling, the system of FICO scores has turned out to be apparently neutral to color, ethnicity, and nationality. Based on bank balances, debts, and payment history, these risk scores defy the social logic of trust in determining the odds that each customer would default on a loan. Let me illustrate with a personal anecdote.

I remember vividly how my American friend was denied a car loan in 1998 because of an error in her student loan database, while I—an immigrant from India on a student visa and graduate fellowship—was granted exactly the same loan. My friend could easily eclipse me on any marker of status or trustworthiness: social and cultural capital, or ethnicity and nationality of consequence. Being an immigrant, my social network was measly, and my accented English only accentuated a yawning cultural deficit; nationally, India was hardly covered in U.S. media at the time, and my ethnicity came in a slightly darker hue, not indicative of a tremendous cultural cachet in the United States; and yet, the banking system trusted my four-year record more than my friend's lifelong sociocultural assets, including citizenship and social networks. It was my first personal realization that physical, social, or cultural history was becoming less effective in presenting an identity that the financial system could trust.*

This crystallization of life into data profiles thus enables a global traffic in identities that could be bought and sold and stolen at a distance. According to Congressional Research Service, "An increase in globalization and a lack of cyber borders provide an environment ripe for identity thieves to operate from within the nation's borders—as well as from beyond. Federal law enforcement is thus challenged with investigating criminals who may or may not be operating within U.S. borders; may have numerous identities—actual, stolen, or cyber; and may be acting alone or as part of a sophisticated criminal enterprise" (Finklea 2012, 1).

Indeed, the release of identities from the shackles of the physical body and social life allows it to be free from life and death. It is estimated that 2.5 million deceased Americans get their identities stolen every year; identity thieves open up new credit lines under the names of the deceased, and new cell phone services. "More than 2,000 identities of corpses per day are assumed by these fraudsters" (ID Analytics 2012, 1).

But identities never truly belonged to the individual to begin with. The "self" is a social process, George Herbert Mead (1913) declared a century ago. For Mead, a person's identity was a misnomer, and multiple personality was in some sense normal, and the often-repeated advice, "be yourself," a strange suggestion. A person was never an identity or a unity. A thinking, unchanging self, separate from others and logically prior to social life, was impossible. Without social interaction, particularly linguistic communication, there would be no self, which was an emergent, dynamic, ongoing social process.

In step with Mead's radical challenge to the idea of a hermetically sealed self, one could ask why lament the unity of identity that was never there? Here we detect differences between social, bureaucratic, and system identi-

---

*One's cultural preparation or social network did matter but only indirectly. One's sociocultural network may be a better predictor of one's success on the job market, which, in theory, could produce conditions for a better credit profile.

ties. While social identity depends on social interactions, and bureaucratic identity on formal institutional membership, system identity crystallizes imperceptibly without one's complete knowledge. One's credit score is constructed and culled from one's myriad financial transactions beyond clear grasp or recognition. One may not fully understand how one's financial identity was created by Experian, for instance, and how it was used by a mortgage broker, landlord, or employer. System identity seems to run parallel to the social self and increasingly neutral to its destiny.

As markers of identity differentiate out of people's physical and social lives, it has become important to safeguard them. Many solutions emerged in the aftermath of the MphasiS-Citibank fraud, ranging from legislative safeguards to technological fixes. But moving back in history to the days when there were no databases of identity to be stolen was not an option. One of the solutions being carried out by the National Software and Services Companies in India is to create more databases, now of Indian employees, carefully recording the details of everyone who works for a global call center, including demographic, educational, and criminal records. What is important to remember is not only that the employees who committed the fraud had no criminal history but also that the possible solution raises the likelihood of thefts by creating more databases of identity. This ever-intensifying dynamic of system identities leads to demands for ever-greater surveillance as a safeguard against potential deviance. Paradoxically, this also spawns the need for countermeasures against data privacy violations. A number of countries have passed legislation on data protection in recent years.

To work with one's system attributes does not mean that one can no longer be social. Indeed, people will always engage in social greetings, there will still be smiles of civil attention, small gestures of help on trains and buses, and in parks and homes; there will still be dating games, furtive glances, tears for the departed, experiences of shame, and the blood rush of sudden desire. The rise of system identities does not herald the death of social identity unless we yield to a false notion of a completely automated world. Indeed, the conflict between system identities and the still operating social and biological forms of existence is often experienced as an awkward dissonance.

## Alarm Clock Dissonance

One way to describe the agent's situation is to employ the imagery of multiple itineraries that a single traveler is asked to follow at once. India's call center agents stand at a crossroads of multiple realms exerting pressures that are at cross-purposes with each other. Their situation provides a mirror in which the rest of us can see ourselves. True, one may argue, no one is a single traveler; everyone is a composite of psychic, social, and biological realms, but a composite that is ever more pushed to travel in different directions. Let me employ an analogy to describe the dissonance of diverse itineraries: the analogy of an alarm clock.

The alarm clock operates on two frontiers at once. On the one hand, it follows the logic of a timetable connecting us to the economic system; the alarm clock wakes one up to catch a flight, which takes one to a business meeting at noon; that is, it connects one to the economic system with its own functional logic of operation, in a network of functional connections; e.g., businesses, employees, and project deadlines, or how the latest iPhone must ship before Christmas to maximize sales, connecting Apple actors with the ordinary consumer in a long chain of systemic integration. On the other hand, the alarm clock also connects to the body through a loud sound, waking the body from its slumber, producing more often than not an experience of shock, a bio-shock. When the alarm clock goes off at its scheduled time in the morning, the body may be in the middle of its deep sleep cycle. The shock of being awakened from delta sleep—the deep, revitalizing, slow-wave kind—is experienced as a bolt from the blue. Hence, the snooze button!

In short, when the clock connects the economic and the biological, the experiential consequence is usually that of dissonance. In its very function, the economic system becomes dysfunctional for the biological realm. The dissonance experienced through two different itineraries, of the market and the body, and their functional logics operating at cross-purposes, is the dissonance of neutrality between different realms. This dissonance—experienced but unrecognized—is what I explore on several fronts in this book. Indian agents, who must work at night to serve the daytime clientele in other parts of the world, are at the forefront of experiencing diverse itineraries of the diurnal body, nocturnal labor, cultural mimicry, neutral accent, and social and system identities. It is not surprising that call centers turn out to be the prime location for exploring the dissonance produced, almost like jet-lag, through connections between realms functionally growing neutral, even antithetical, to each other.

At times the dissonance originates from problems of human-machine interface. As global communication lacks physical proximity, it depends heavily on customer relations databases, which are integrated into the process of making calls through dialer software programs, targeting select database profiles. For example, if Tarun sold mortgages, the dialer would not dial old-age or poor-credit profiles, that is, profiles that were unlikely candidates for a loan. However, the machine-dialed conversation was not free from contingencies.

"There was this interesting incident . . . ," Tarun offered an example. "People say I have a gift of gab but this was the first time I couldn't answer. He was an old guy, he just picked up the phone. I had to sell him the same thing. I had to ask whether he wanted a swimming pool in his house . . . The moment they want a swimming pool, they need a loan and we are there to provide them a loan. So we were going to put needs into his head . . . but he answered, see, I am blind and I am eighty. I have a house. . . . What will I do with a swimming pool? Why do I need a swimming pool? I don't need a swimming pool," his voice rising to a crescendo of annoyance. Tarun could only mutter, "Thank you, sir."

Such dialer-originated calls to wrong profiles were as common as the ones to correct profiles. It was clear that these global conversations were not between persons; they were not even conversations in the regular sense. They were instances of communication between personas or ghosts in the machine in which actual persons found themselves unwittingly implicated, providing the necessary fuel for the economic system to conduct itself. When conversations moved in the social arena, as we see in the case of the blind customer, social identity disrupted system identity, demonstrating how system profiles, quite often, were poor constructions.

Disjunctures in global communication often led to failed conversations, or worse, no conversation when two parties, as I heard frequently on the floor, talked past each other. Mostly economic in nature, these failures were marked, and indeed, countable in telemarketing or collection calls through the differences in average revenue generated by each caller every month. On several occasions, I was informed how American companies did not renew contracts with their Indian call centers on perceived deficiencies of "quality," which probably stood for failures of communication. Yet, failures aside, GoCom-like call centers have been sufficiently successful to register a dramatic rise in the last decade, and the new global communicative regime has become an undeniable reality. Allow me to explain the systemic basis of the new regime with a brief theoretical detour to the notion of *algocracy* (Aneesh 2006).

In the absence of system identities, there would be no identity theft of the kind we are witnessing today. There would be no identity protection industry and no legislation that has evolved around it. There would also be no software dialers designed to target specific identities or profiles to sell a mortgage or mobile connection. The role of dialers in the call center industry is increasingly important, for it forms the connection between a calling agent and the target profile, all managed by a set of algorithms. Indeed, profiles themselves are constructed through a different set of algorithms.

I have described dialers as part of *algocracy* in an article (Aneesh 2009), a new system of governance that I distinguish from two other forms of organization—bureaucracy and the market, each guided by different ruling principles: bureaucracy (legal-rational), the market (price), and algocracy (programming or algorithm). To give a small, everyday example, when we fill in the "fields" on a computer screen, we often cannot type in the wrong part of a form, or put the address in the space for the phone number for the field may be coded to accept only numbers, not text; similarly, an agent cannot choose to dial a profile (unless, of course, they eschew the dialer and dial manually). The embedded code provides existing channels that guide action in precise ways.

With sufficient bandwidth, labor in Indian firms have been systemically linked to corporate sites across the globe, reducing the spatial gulf to a matter of good or bad connection. How does one make sense of this development? Is this a new kind of bureaucratic integration (intrafirm) whereby workers located in faraway places can work without physically crossing the borders? Or, is this market integration (interfirm), a new form of international trade, confirming an old economic principle that if a service is produced at a lower cost by another firm or country, it makes no economic sense to produce it domestically? Relying on the work of Coase (1937), economic analyses tend to confine themselves to these two alternatives of bureaucracy and market: "either a firm makes a component itself (bureaucratic governance) or it buys it from an autonomous supplier (market governance)" (Williamson 1981). Thus, firms emerge when transaction costs of market contracting exceed those of bureaucratic governance.

Both alternatives, however, fail to fully capture the emergent reality of call center work or global software development. While the bureaucratic model may loosely be applied in cases of subsidiaries (e.g., Microsoft U.S.A. and Microsoft India), there is rarely any bureaucratic integration possible for global projects due not only to distance but also to country-specific labor regulations. It is difficult to have a single managerial structure to govern different teams located in different regions of the world.

One may then be tempted to suggest that it is a simple case of market-based outsourcing where the market replaces bureaucracy as a governance mechanism. Instead of doing everything in-house, the medium of money is used to attach a price to the works of different teams around the globe—a practice captured in terms of trade. The market ends up governing these projects by driving inefficient firms out of business. While this argument is valid regarding the dimension of price-based subcontracting, it fails to account for its collaborative character focused on the same software project or telemarketing campaign. These are not discrete exchanges conducted at arm's length presupposed in market transactions but collaborative ones on a shared project often with a single deadline. Neither the market (discrete transactions) nor bureaucracy (managerial oversight) is sufficient to explain the organizational reality of globally distributed software development or call center communication.

The third way, network forms of organization (Powell 1990), captures quite well the initial phase—the formation of initial business ties—of this practice, but it, too, covers only a minor aspect of the collaborative software development and call center communication. The question arises: what additional organizational mechanisms inform the emergence of collaborative projects at the global level occurring in real-time? Who manages these joint projects? This is where we can identify an additional system of governance, termed algocracy.

The thesis of algocracy is about the substantive consequences of technical decision making. Let's look at the classic example of assembly line systems where the machinery itself is made to direct the labor process and set the pace from factories to fast-food joints (Braverman 1974; Edwards 1979; Leidner 1993), or how a nonhuman structure like the speed bump (a sleeping cop) contains within it a "motive," delegating a social rule to a device (Latour 1994), or the prioritization of music in octaves by the volt-per-octave standard adopted in the Moog synthesizer (Pinch and Trocco 2004). In all of these cases, initial technological decisions regarding assembly lines, speed bump, or volt-per-octave standard lead to important social consequences. Algocracy clearly privileges higher-level executives whose preferences may be preprogrammed in its platforms. However, I would like to extend the thesis of code beyond its local uses—technical control in organizations—in order to characterize it as a generalized medium like money, with equally far-reaching implications. Code emerges in this account as a language with money-like liquidity, acting as the medium of different kinds of things: audio, visual, monetary, and ahem, identity (Aneesh 2006). The genealogy of algocracy could be traced as far back as the proposal by Gottfried Leibniz, a seventeenth-century philosopher and mathematician, to build machines for deducing valid references through a "calculus of reason" (*calculus ratiocinator*). Despite the long history of symbolic logic, it was not until the cold-war-related American defense strategies that programming acquired its practical importance (Abbate 1999; Aneesh 2001).

To distinguish algocracy from bureaucratic and market systems, let me extend the insights available in theories of differentiation and self-referential systems (Alexander and Colomy 1990; Luhmann 1984). Modern bureaucracy—as Max Weber (1921) detected—operated on the basis of a legal-rational code that reduced the discretionary power of office holders. Unlike previous bureaucracies of Egypt, China, and medieval Europe that employed old modes of trust and hierarchies of Stände, Weber discerned the primacy of juridical formalism in modern bureaucratic systems. While scholars have questioned the Weberian thesis by showing how real bureaucracies were fraught with informal relationships and how formal rules were often inefficient and dysfunctional (Merton 1968; Selznick 1980), they confused between the system's internal code and environmental pressures: for a system to increase its internal complexity it must be open to environmental stimulations (e.g., by social life), but it must perform its operations in its own language through its own code. While social and informal action has crucial bearing on a bureaucratic system, informality is not the code by which action could be legitimized within bureaucratic systems. A firm manager may recruit her nephew or friend as an employee, but she must not justify the recruitment on the basis of kinship or friendship norms; she must present her decision in terms of merit and credentials. Indeed, norms of kinship and friendship are recoded as nepotism and cronyism in bureaucratic organizations. While kinship and friendship networks may exist in real bureaucracies, they lose their validity basis with the ethical neutralization of lifeworld perspectives.

Similarly, market systems may also be informed by social networks (Granovetter 1985), yet the market behaves as a differentiated system precisely because it no longer operates through social code despite its apparent embeddedness in social life. Luhmann (1984) resolves, if only implicitly, the dilemma of embedded and disembedded action through a unique strategy:

once a system differentiates and turns autonomous (or gets disembedded), it becomes a recursively closed circuit of communication, delimiting itself from its environment in a self-referential manner. This does not imply that the economic system operates in a social vacuum. The informal social world acts as the presupposed and necessary environment for the economic system, which constructs itself from moment to moment by creating a boundary between itself and its environment. It responds to the changes occurring in its environment by registering those perturbations in its own language. A friendly social alliance may operate in the market system, but it must eventually be reduced through the code of payment/nonpayment to be part of market transactions; otherwise, we will have to define it as part of the social system of gift exchange, not market exchange.

Following field theory (Martin 2003, 2011), we can avoid the language of causation where one variable, element, or system directly affects the behavior of another. Instead of mechanistic determination by an external agent, we can argue that market systems build their complexity in a self-referential manner from an array of stimulations—social, political, legal, scientific, or psychic— that must be converted into the system's own language for them to be meaningful. Harry's desire for a cold, refreshing carbonated drink on a hot summer day may be seen as a psychosomatic or cultural need but his desire is registered by the market system only as a specific consumer demand, which can be meaningful to the system not in psychosomatic but in economic terms.

An algocratic system consists of programming schemes embedded in software platforms that structure possible forms of work performance. This system governs work through the design of the work process itself. It would be wrong to assume that algocracy merely dresses up bureaucratic rules in the software medium, and delegates them to a code-based device, which merely implements those rules on the fly. Algocracy is not bureaucracy for a clear reason: there is no common metalanguage shared by bureaucratic (legal code) and algocratic (binary code) systems of governance. Imperatives of programming are not bureaucratic but mathematical even while a programmer codes bureaucratic controls in a software system.

Algocracy may encode not only bureaucratic but also nonbureaucratic, less hierarchical governance as seen in peer-to-peer programming schemes or open-source development projects. The notion of algocracy thus implies "rule of the algorithm" or "rule of the code." Earlier I misrecognized algocracy as "hyper-bureaucracy" (Aneesh 1999), which was also misrecognized as perfect law by Lessig (1999). While bureaucracy and algocracy may be the necessary environments for each other, the two systems of governance are structurally open but operationally closed, to borrow Niklas Luhmann's (1984) phrase. One can detect its structural openness in managerial insistence on replicating the previous work structure into software systems despite systems analysts' contention about their inefficiencies. But when algocracy negotiates bureaucratic imperatives in its own language, it transforms them.

To separate the two from the commonly used action-theoretic perspective, bureaucratic governance is internally dependent on both action orientation, requiring people to learn and embody the authority of laws, rules and regulations, and action consequence when sanctions steer action through functional consequences. In bureaucracy, rule adherence is managed through socialization or training (action orientation), integrating the demands of rules into one's behavior, which acquires the willingness to distinguish between permissible and nonpermissible action. An added mechanism to ensure proper organizational behavior is incentive, which in its negative (penalty) and positive (reward) forms drives action through its consequences. Market systems, on the other hand, require only action consequence to guide behavior through a price-based spur to action. In contrast, algocratic systems do not need either action orientation or consequence to coordinate action. Programming technologies seek to structure the possible field of action without a similar need for orienting people toward learning the legal rules. Action is controlled neither by socializing workers into regulatory demands, nor by punishing workers for their failure, but by shaping an environment in which there are only programmed alternatives to performing the work. Thus, work involves a lower focus on the knowledge of regulations and a greater stress on the ability to use a software program.

The notion of algocracy suggests that authority does not need legitimacy in the same sense, because either there are no alternative routes to the permissible ones or the permissible routes are themselves programmed. There is no comparison that can be used to delegitimize authority, which is increasingly embedded in the underlying code, rendering the hierarchical system of authority relations less useful. This is not to suggest that bureaucratic structures and rules have disappeared in the global firm; both systems may indeed exist simultaneously: the call center's internal structure may still look bureaucratic if less hierarchical, while its communicative work may be managed through algocratic mechanisms. Table 4.1 is a stylized comparison to capture the ways in which bureaucratic, monetary, and algocratic systems are different from each other:

Table 4.1 Systems of Organization

| Key Features | Bureaucratic | Market | Algocratic |
|---|---|---|---|
| Governance | Written rules (legal positivism) | Price | Program |
| Code | Permissible/ not permissible | Payment/ nonpayment | True/False (1/0) |
| Medium | Routines | Money | Programming language |
| Labor Integration | Hierarchical | N/A (only indirect) | Network |

Whereas bureaucratic governance, as Weber (1921) has noted, is conducted through juridical formalism with associated rules and regulations, market exchange is governed through price with only two options: whether to buy the product and how much of it to buy. Algocratic governance, on the other hand, as explained earlier, is coded as a program, which automatically determines the range of possible action. In terms of operational code, bureaucracy operates by the permissibility or nonpermissibility of action according to written rules. While there may be ambiguity about the permissibility of a certain course of action, the ambiguity is usually solved by either making the rules clearer and more specific, or by incorporating the ambiguous as a version of the already defined. For a market event, the action must follow the code of payment or nonpayment, as all market transactions to be called as such must be accomplished through some sort of payment (Luhmann 1984).

In contrast, algocratic systems use the logical code of truth values defined as true-not true or, more conventionally, 1 or 0 for their organizational constitution and complexity. For systemic communication, algocracies use the medium of programming language in contrast to the use of money by market systems and of routines by bureaucracies. In terms of labor integration, hierarchical membership seems crucial to bureaucracies while the market integrates labor only indirectly (e.g., labor market). Algocracy, on the other hand, appears to connect through the structure of computer networks.

Much of real-time call center–based customer service work across continents is managed algocratically through various software systems, including dialer software and customer relations management (CRM) systems. In Gurgaon's call centers, customer service work usually began with customers' interaction with a voice-activated algocratic system, which routed outbound telemarketing calls based on customer profiles and directed inbound calls toward departments or employee skills (using computer voice toward systematically preprogrammed and numbered options). To match and organize multitype customers and multiskilled agents, various queuing models and algorithms were used in the software for operating skills–based routing of calls within a call center. These algocratic systems may or may not work efficiently for the organization or its customers, but their use has become pervasive.

## The Dialer

For outbound calls, GoCom managed the agent-customer interaction algocratically. In most cases, as mentioned earlier, it was not the agent who dialed the phone number. It was the dialer software that targeted specific profiles from customer databases with strict parameters covering credit history, buying habits, and such demographic variables as age, gender, income, region, and education while also handling the do-not-call (DNC) list. When Geeta sold mortgages to potential customers in the United States, the dialer skipped the profiles that were unlikely candidates for a loan, according to a mathematical configuration.

The dialer resembled an assembly line production system at least in one respect: the pace of work was designed in the program itself. Raj, a twenty-two-year-old agent, complained: "The dialer tells you to take the break . . . You get a break around 7 and you get a break around 9 for half an hour . . . And you are supposed to be logged in for at least 7 hours 45 minutes, overall. Because if you suddenly want to go to the loo, it just cuts down on your time." On an average, the dialer paced the work of agents by dialing 250–300 calls a night, requiring the agent to be always prepared for a possible conversation. At GoCom, I witnessed both old-fashioned, manual dialing as well as algocratically managed dialing using the automatic dialer whose use dominated the work.

"There are two types of sales. Dialer and manual," Mukul explained, "Manual you get the leads from somewhere, from your TL [team leader] . . ."

In personal conversations, Mukul switched back and forth deciding between them. "With dialer, it's very difficult to make a sale, I'd rather have manual calling; the leads are good . . . you can make sales because if you call ten existing customers, at least one customer will renew the contract." But quickly within the same conversation, Mukul extolled the virtues of the dialer. "Yesterday the CEO came and said, try to cut down on manual calling, you'll kill yourself, dialers are the best way to make sales," Mukul agreed. "That is also fine because I am not quite comfortable with manual. They gave me two-day manual dialing, but I did not find it comfortable. Because it takes a lot of time."

"I am doing manual dialing right now." Sanjay confirmed that manual dialing required labor. "I've done it before also, but it's very, you know, very labor oriented . . . you have to remember the name and number and all . . . and then you have to dial, like, three times that number." Perhaps both kinds of dialing are hard because it is just difficult to make a sale in a telemarketing campaign and the pressure keeps mounting.

"They are putting too much pressure, [new agents] have to perform in the first week . . . it's not going to be possible, because there are guys who are, even after a year, still finding it difficult to make sales on the dialer . . . Once you get into the manual dialer, your skill is totally ruined." Mukul told a story of manual dialing, "Once Abhishek gave me a trade lead but he was so cute. Not cute, I mean . . . he said if you make two sales, give me one sale. Actually I made one sale . . . but after the dialer . . . I said, I'm not going to dial manually . . . you can just dial . . . if you find it comfortable, ok you can do. I'm not finding comfortable in manual." Manual dialing, most agents thought, was not a permanent solution.

"If you are looking for short term or you are just looking for targets, ok I need five or ten sales, you can go for manual, that is fine," Mukul said. But the growing ability of automatic dialers seemed to signal the future trend of outbound calls and all telemarketing campaigns because automatic dialers were informed by an algorithm-based predictive dialing, which has grown more sophisticated since this research in 2004–5.

The programming scheme of the dialer is increasingly based on predictive algorithms, ensuring that agents contact only live parties, discarding busy numbers, disconnected lines, and fax or answering machines. Although I found that GoCom's dialer kept bumping into answering machines, the ability of predictive dialers to distinguish between an answering machine and a live person has since raised productivity by reducing the time wasted on busy signals, invalid numbers, and answering machines. But it has also intensified the agent's time use. Predictive dialers tend to dial ahead of the agent's actual availability, queuing up busy signals for automatic redial. In manual dialing, agents could relax and sit idle if the calls dialed ran into answering machines or babysitters.

"We get to speak only ten to fifteen people in a day. Only live voice. Otherwise . . . answering machines because they not at home, they're at work," Sanjay complained about the dialer at his call center. Did he leave messages on answering machines? "No, we're not allowed to," Sanjay said, "and even if someone picks up the phone, they're most likely not the contact, they are gatekeepers . . . like the babysitter or anyone we can't speak with . . . So [real contacts] we get rarely and when we do, they also hang up on us." Frustrating as it might have been for him to deal with the gatekeepers, it was a less functional and thus less intense experience.

The predictive dialer, in theory, has enabled a work regime that connects the agents with live parties most of the time. All advanced predictive dialers algocratically control the ratio of calls to agents, altering their dialing rate according to the number of connections made while also adjusting to the behavior of the ongoing telemarketing campaign. The dialer generates statistics about each agent's current and average call connection time for previous days and locations dialed. At GoCom, the rudimentary form of this system was already present. While it was certainly demanding on the agent, it also resulted in nuisance for the customer, who on occasion might hear only silence when the dialer made more calls than agents could handle.

Let us now take a brief look at how dialers are actually and potentially linked to profiles, specters, and ghosts of actual people, to system constructions that the dialer in turn is programmed to call, enmeshing actual persons in a possible conversation.

## Functional Personhood: Social, Bureaucratic, and System Identity

In sociology and anthropology, as mentioned earlier, identity has never been a completely personal matter. Social identity is an identity continually renegotiated through linguistic interactions and social performances (Cerulo 1997). The sense of self emerges from dialogues with others, from experiences and exchanges involving gestures and languages. To such experiences, we can add interactions with places. A great deal of anthropology and philosophy has devoted itself to place and its connection with identity and memory (Appadurai 1988; Augé 1995; Bachelard 1964; de Certeau 1984; Feld and Basso 1996; Ferguson and Gupta 1992). Smells, vistas, and sounds—linguistic and nonlinguistic—of a place have been recognized as crucial to developing a sense of self. Feld (1996), for instance, has explained how sound is central to Kahuli experience and orientation in the Bosavi forests, and how senses make place and places make senses. While the notion of anthropological place with connotations of a self-contained whole is largely a reality invented by inhabitants as well as scholars, it has been a useful invention: "land has been cultivated, nature domesticated, reproductions of the generations ensured" (Augé 1995). Such places relate to the concrete and symbolic construction of space of identity, social cohesion, and clear historical memory.

System identity, on the other hand, is a relatively recent development. One can trace its early development to the creation of what we may call bureaucratic identity, resulting from the modern state's attempts to make a society legible for taxation, conscription, and governance. Political scientist James Scott (1998) explains how the modern state started such disparate processes as the creation of permanent last names, population registers, the establishment of cadastral surveys, the standardization of language and law. The premodern state, on the other hand, was "partially blind," Scott informs us, "it knew precious little about its subjects, their wealth, their landholdings and yields, their location, their very identity . . . As a result its interventions were often crude and self-defeating" (1998, 2). But modern states have not only organized population in a way that simplifies their functions internally, they have also expropriated from people, as John Torpey (1999) pointed out, the legitimate "means of movement," across international boundaries.

Over time bureaucratic identity gained ascriptive state-provided apparels of passports, birth certificates, and driver's licenses. Now we acquire, show, and swipe a variety of ID cards at a variety of gates, doors, and desks for a variety of agencies: corporations, governments, and municipalities. Modern bureaucracies have long constructed our identities tailored for their own functioning, a construction to which we responded by adapting or maladapting to them. Modern national identity, for instance, has not been a simple construction of the state; citizens responded to the construction through active identification with, and loyalty toward, an imagined community.

But system identity is slightly different from bureaucratic identity as its workings take place in the background. It multiplies for the purposes of economic, medical, financial, and judicial systems, setting up individuals' behavioral records for systemic needs. Tucked away in databases, system identities are at a remove from everyday experience but they do exert a certain pressure: a low credit score signals that I need to tighten my belt in order to stay creditworthy, similar to a financial warning by a relative or a parent in the realm of social identity. But I cannot "experience" the abstract logic of system identity in the same sense, or form a relationship with it, even if the warning floats out of my computer as human voice, and scholars write about its very real effects (Nass and Brave 2005). It is an identity created solely for the purpose and health of another system; it is functional for the system but not necessarily for the person.

I must caution that this division between social, bureaucratic, and the systemic, while pragmatic, has unresolved semantic knots because the social can be observed as a system while systems—legal, economic, scientific, political—are all social products. Distinctions among social, bureaucratic, and system identities are therefore distinctions within the social. This differentiation allows me to highlight the fanning out of social identity into functionally defined system identities. By system identity I hope to highlight a kind of identity to which the person has made no direct contribution, even as system identities are constructed from moment to moment by feeding on the behavioral expressions of socially formed personality.

Conventionally, one's identity—based on ethnicity, nationality, kinship, language, sexuality, or work—results from an interaction between the person and social structure; both shape and are shaped by the other to the point where it is difficult to give a complete description of either in isolation. Often, it is not a given *identity*, but a work in progress, *identification*, denoting a conscious participation of persons. With the development of system identity, however, it becomes a one-sided affair where the person's contribution is mostly a passive one. One is no longer emotionally or cognitively mobilized in identifying practices; rather, one becomes a recipient of multiple identities. Various systems catch the person unawares, using her changing behavior as fodder to fuel an internal systemic dynamic. However, we must not understand system identity as a mere machine enterprise. One could certainly gain awareness of the system, and change one's behavior in a way that directly changes one's system identity.

The second difference from bureaucratic identity lies in divergent goals for identity construction. Passports, birth certificates, and other forms of identification are attempts at constructing fixed, ascriptive personhood.

Their motive is to ensure that the person is essentially the same through various changes in personality, body, behavior, and being. They make sure that the person flying to New Delhi today is the one who was issued the passport a decade ago. The motive is to fix the person in their essence despite their multiple mercurial appearances, to privilege being over becoming.

I use system identities to denote the opposite. Here the goal of identity construction is to capture constant change in what seems like an unchanging self. It reflects the movement from bureaucratic to algocratic constructions of identity, from analog to digital, static to malleable data, and what Negroponte (1995) called "atoms to bits." Identities are no longer fixed; they keep changing with the person. There is no permanent credit score for a person's financial identity, no permanent health record for their medical identity, or permanent political identity as a voter. Yet, with every credit card purchase, every wish list, every loan and repayment, one's financial identity is being constantly reconstructed without the person's conscious participation. All that is solid melts into a river of change. System identities do not portray finished being; they portray passing, from day to day, minute to minute. They privilege becoming over being. In order to know a person requires knowing, not how one has remained the same, but how one has changed over time, and more important, how one will change in the future. It becomes important to know not only where one is stationed but where one moves about.

As I sip tea while revising this manuscript in a Cafe Coffee Day in New Delhi on this bright January morning, I have already left traces of my behavior, unintentionally, on globally mobile systems. My iPhone has kept track of my movement from home to the coffee shop where I arrived at 10:37 AM; my CapitalOne credit card knows that I continue to use it in India more on caffeine than mango juice; Airtel, the Indian cell phone company, has records of my 3G data use; and Amazon knows my changing taste in books while Google and the U.S. Government understand the rest about which I don't have the faintest idea. Well, we have some idea, as the American Civil Liberties Union uncovered a court document about a drug investigation conducted by U.S. Immigration and Customs Enforcement, containing detailed information federal agents were able to extract from one suspect's iPhone after cracking the four-character numeric PIN in minutes: call logs, text and chat data, contacts, installed applications, stored voicemails, passwords, and IP connection data, 659 geolocation points, including 227 cell towers and 403 WiFi networks with which the cell phone had connected (Soghoian and Gilens 2013).

As opposed to government surveillance, I installed a little widget on my computer recently to track who was tracking me. The results were impressive; I was quite sought after. Here is the breakup: *Advertising*: 661 trackers, with the sole purpose of delivering advertisements; *Analytics*: 251 trackers for the purpose of providing research and analytics to website publishers; *Beacons*: 282 trackers, serving no purpose other than tracking (beacons, conversion pixels, audience segmentation pixels, etc.); *Privacy*: 18 trackers, for privacy notices and other related elements; *Widgets*: 149 trackers, providing page functionality (social network buttons, comment form, etc.).

The enormous scale of state surveillance exposed by Edward Snowden in 2013 only confirms the importance of data, and destinies tied to it, in world society. Since the publication of *Discipline and Punish* (Foucault 1979), the most cited work in the humanities and social sciences, there has emerged a body of scholarship that has further analyzed and theorized—particularly in the wake of new technologies—the problem of surveillance (Lyon 1994; Marx 1989). With the digital turn in technologies, the focus has shifted to dataveillance and biometrics with a concern for administration, social sorting, and simulation that take place independently of persons (Haggerty and Ericson 2000; Lyon 2002; Simon 2005). The notion of system identity resonates well with the above scholarship. However, my concern in this book is less with surveillance and more with functional differentiation of personal attributes: how the minute-by-minute log of my behavior could be used to construct dynamic and multiple system profiles that make me available for a host of different purposes, creating highly effective identities, some of which could be stolen.

Following Mead's dictum that a multiple personality is in a certain sense normal, my multiple system identities are continually constructed for the sake of advertisers, banks, phone companies, stores, hospitals, insurance companies, pharmaceutical industry, and a thousand others. Not only have I multiple identities—and here is the twist—they don't really belong to me. I do not have property rights over this profile. People cannot lay claim to their intimate itineraries prepared by function systems. Generating data amenable to real-time configuration and prediction, such constructions of mine inform the world better than any conscious effort on my part. Our "digital droppings" become proprietary business records, Deibert (2013, 56) points out, and companies see our intentions, hopes, and habits as resources to be tapped and harvested. There is a sudden growth of companies like mushrooms of all shapes and sizes, systematically examining the big data, passing them around, developing algorithms to make the data speak for different purposes.

"Late in the past century, to come up with this level of reporting, the East German government had to enlist tens of thousands of its citizens as spies," Baker (2008, 14) notes, "Today, we spy on ourselves and send electronic updates minute by minute . . . We don't have to participate or even know that our mathematical ghosts are laboring night and day as lab rats."

Specters of global communication, as I referred to these ghosts in a 2007 article (Aneesh 2007), reside on both sides of the equation. As call center workers train and learn to change into a self that is sufficiently neutral, free from regional accents and native cultural traits, their customers in the West are already available in their spectral form through their system identities. While call center agents must be consciously mobilized in culture work, the rest of us are being constructed without our direct knowledge. As the *New York Times* reported, "You can be sold in . . . milliseconds . . . On the Web, powerful algorithms are sizing you up, based on myriad data points . . . Then, in real time, the chance to show you an ad is auctioned to the highest bidder. Not that you'd know it . . . all of this happens automatically, and imperceptibly, to most consumers . . . Real-time bidding creates the possibility for companies to tag you wherever you are going, without you knowing or having the ability to influence it . . . It is becoming a huge imbalance for the ordinary user because, in the end, the ordinary user is the product" (Singer 2012).

The result is a collage of multiple selves, unhinged, constructed, and tracked separately by different function systems. We may have a holistic image of ourselves, somewhat frozen in time, but function systems combine and construct us from the shards of our everyday life, from our continuous exertion and sweat, creating myriad mirrors and capturing divergent reflections of personality from moment to moment. One is converted into functionally separated components for different purposes. One's financial, medical, political, personal, and employment identities are constructed and further split into multiple ways. My financial identity itself has multiplied into my being an actual and potential customer, actual and potential borrower, actual and potential investor. Vast databases of behavior, action, and bodily changes allow algocratic systems to come up with complex mathematical models of past and future behavior.

Just as credit scores profile our financial identity, efforts are on to create measures of work identity or the value of one's skill set, not in a static but in a dynamic way. Such an identity would change as the person ages. For baseball players, WAR—wins above replacement—score, a nonstandardized statistic, has been developed, for instance, to mark their value—current and future. Modeling aging bodies, skills, and their current form in the equation, WAR claims to represent how many more wins a player would offer a team as opposed to his replacement level by a minor league player at that position. Workers, so measured, may rise and fall with the scores attached to them just like an individual's financial profile or creditworthiness rises and falls with one's credit score. It's quite likely that dynamic work profiles will eventually replace the static models of one's ability, skills, and knowledge. "And for these quantified masses, the security of the flock fades away," writes Baker (2008). "After all, each lazy or incompetent worker who survives in the mathematically assessed workplace represents a market inefficiency. Once the measurements are in place, these workers will presumably plunge in value or be purged, just like an underperforming stock in a portfolio."

One's identity as a shopper is already quite sophisticated. Online stores not only keep records of what one clicks on their site, where one lingers, how much one spends, what advertisements one notices; they also use algorithms to profile every individual with a view to directing future products at them. Algocratic systems monitor one's monetary contribution to the store and calculate what one is likely to purchase in the future. They seek to unearth from every purchase not only one's capacity to spend from a given income but also one's taste, lifestyle, family structure, demographic location, and participation in their tribe as marketers articulate it, a tribe of strangers with similar taste, lifestyle, and consumption habits. Shall we call it a virtual tribe that is further reproduced through various incentives and seductions? One's shopping behavior—diet, clothing, brand loyalty—has clues to those parts of one's personality that one may not be aware of oneself, but they are crucial to the construction of one's shopping identity.

With an algocratically constructed shopping identity at hand, the system generates electronic coupons and incentives on the fly to manipulate behavior in real time. IBM and Springboard Networks have developed, for example, smart wireless-enabled shopping carts with mini computers on board, allowing customers to search for products, scan items, see instantly generated, targeted sales in their aisle, pay, and leave without waiting at the checkout counter. Once deployed, smart shopping carts are supposed to reduce the store's labor costs while allowing advertisers to connect directly with highly specific shopping identities. The promise of success aside, the final frontier in shopping algorithms may be to link up one's proclivities for certain foods and one's genomic identity, being mapped out on a separate bio-logical register. Potentially, food can be designed for this tribe of strangers that shares a genetic makeup.

Genetic databases coupled with constant monitoring of behavior are helping form a medical identity without one's awareness of its implications. Potentially, one's genetic makeup, food purchases, and hospital visits may all be combined into an ever-changing medical identity. Smokers already pay 14 percent higher average monthly premium than the premium paid by non-smokers in the United States, and the monthly premium paid by obese men based on their Body Mass Index (BMI) is 29 percent higher than the average premium paid by men in the normal category (eHealth 2013).

Efforts are on to register minute to minute changes in our bodies. A range of bio-nano-sensors are being developed for a remote monitoring of bodies and behavior. Continuous monitoring of humans for glucose has already reached the market (Valgimigli et al. 2010), and the real-time remote moni-toring of blood pressure in mice through a wireless microsystem has been demonstrated (Cong et al. 2009). Tests have been conducted for bio-nano-sensors to detect single-metabolites like glucose, lactate, glutamate, and adenosine triphosphate, using an electrochemical front-end made with off-the-shelf components, a radio frequency communication subsystem, and an antenna (Carrara et al. 2011).

These bio-nano-sensors are quite different from the body's natural nano-sensors, for instance, our sense of smell for nanosize molecules. The con-struction of a world by the body is quite different from the construction of a world by a function system, a topic I explore in chapter 5. Further, experi-ments are being conducted, for example, to put a web of monitors under the kitchen tiles that can dispatch information wirelessly about each visit by an elderly person to the kitchen, his or her changing weight or patterns of movement and speech, or send an alert if he or she fails to walk into the kitchen one day (Baker 2008). Only algocratic systems can govern and sift through these data, now termed "big data," winnowing signal from noise, with customized algorithms for the disabled and the elderly.

The list of system identities is long and growing. Perhaps it was in the 1990s that system identities staged a silent coup in the United States. In order to matter in social life, one had to work with one's system profiles. The emergence of system or data profiles has neither been smooth nor seamless. They are not without their experiential shocks and felt disjunctures. But they have infiltrated even the most social of activities: finding a romantic partner.

There are systems that are busy sizing one up as a potential match for another. From eHarmony to OK Cupid, algorithms are being continuously developed and refined to offer us our next romantic partner, and potentially, family.

Constructions of identities may be harmless in themselves, but these multiple functional selves built by different systems at times may exert pressures on us that are at cross purposes with each other. Disjunctures in social and system identities are already noticed in such risks as the financial identity theft we noticed in the MphasiS-Citibank fraud case, or an increased incidence of medical identity theft that raises the premiums for its victims, about half of whom lose coverage entirely. The development and functional differentiation of personhood may allow contradictory pressures to develop while reducing the possibility for coherent resistance. Call centers offer us a microcosm of the emerging clashes in differentiated life. Let me use the nighttime economy of call centers to illustrate in chapter 5 the fault lines developing between the diurnal body, nocturnal labor, and a world economy neutral to day and night differences.

5

*Nightly Clashes:* Diurnal Body, Nocturnal Labor, Neutral Markets

For quite some time I have been intrigued by a puzzle: Why is there a total absence, in thought and in practice, of any collective struggle against the graveyard shift worldwide? Why do we notice widespread indifference toward nocturnal labor, given the undeniable diurnal makeup of the human body? Are we just happy to have a job, any job, day or night? Remember, we have not always been so neutral to long hours of work. From *Daily Telegraph* of January 17, 1860, Karl Marx (2004, 132) quoted at length the shame expressed by a county magistrate over long working hours, "Children of nine or ten years are dragged from their squalid beds at two, three, or four o'clock in the morning and compelled to work for a bare subsistence until ten, eleven, or twelve at night, their limbs wearing away, their frames dwindling . . . What can be thought of a town which holds a public meeting to petition that the period of labour for men shall be diminished to eighteen hours a day?"

Those grueling work hours did not go unchallenged. The twenties and thirties rumbled with strikes for reduced work hours and demands for a ten-hour day in many industrial towns of the nineteenth-century United States.

The Workingmen's Advocate reported during the bakers' strike in New York in 1834: "journeymen employed in the loaf bread business have for years been suffering worse than Egyptian bondage. They have had to labor on an average of eighteen to twenty hours out of the twenty-four" (Trachtenberg and Weinstone 1931, 1). The International Workingmen's Association declared its demand for an eight-hour day at its Geneva convention in August 1866: "The legal limitation of the working day is a preliminary condition without which all future attempts and improvements and emancipation of the working class must prove abortive . . . The congress proposes eight hours as the legal limit of the working day" (Foner 1986, 12).

In the United States, the eight-hour day became the focus of the Chicago labor movement in 1864. The Federation of Organized Trades and Labor Unions at its Chicago convention in 1884 made its demands clear: "eight hours shall constitute a legal day's labour from and after May 1, 1886, and that we recommend to labour organizations throughout this jurisdiction that they so direct their laws as to conform to this resolution by the time named." By the mid-eighties, the movement for the shorter workday for all other employees culminated in a massive wave of May Day strikes. Probably, a half million workers joined the eight-hour agitation, and crippling strikes and demonstrations shook large and small cities as well as rural towns. Chicago witnessed the most intense May Day with nearly 90,000 street demonstrators and 30,000–40,000 on strike with every railroad in the city paralyzed, all the freight houses shut, and most of the industries brought to a standstill (Foner 1986, 27). Some workers won a shorter eight- or nine-hour workday with no pay reduction; others negotiated pay cuts with the reduction in hours.

In short, before World War II workers agitated for a shorter workday with greater intensity than they did for higher wages (Whaples 1990). The origin of May Day is inextricably bound up with the struggle for the shorter workday, a defining attribute of labor politics in the United States from the beginning of the factory system. Why don't we see similar struggles against night work? In the last decade and a half, we have witnessed many struggles from Seattle to Madison to New York, but none against labored nights.

Perhaps the concern about long working hours is qualitatively different from the one about night work. After all, if one works eight hours at night, one can rest during the day. Work and rest cycles, one may contend, are more important for a person than day and night cycles. As early as 1817 Robert Owen propounded the thesis of "Eight hours labour, Eight hours recreation, Eight hours rest," highlighting the importance of time, not the time of day, the weight of quantity, not quality. Since the nineteenth century, time seems to have acquired space-like qualities. While remaining invisible and irrevocable, time started being cut up like a thing, and then quantified in a way that allowed one hour to be equivalent to another. Since the invention of the electric bulb, the qualitative difference between day and night, dawn and dusk has been reduced to private experience with a minor role in organizing life, and the relationship of light-dark cycles to the body's circadian rhythms has lost some of its relevance.

In everyday experience, however, day and night matter very much. Travelers routinely avoid taking cheaper red eye and early morning flights. Jet lag, like the alarm clock dissonance, is a direct experience of a break between the circadian clock and day and night cycles. Still, for me, the question of night work was perplexing only in theory and occasional personal experiences until I started working at GoCom. The experience of working at night made me understand in a new light what other agents were saying about their work in general. The problem of night work seemed to color their entire life. It was curious for me to realize that their complaints were not directed against night work per se, yet I could easily glean from their seemingly general complaints an array of anxieties that led, in a diffused form, to the problem of night work. Their complaints renewed my attention to the puzzle. What prevented these agents, and the public, from recognizing the travails of night work? Escaping clear perception, the problem of night work took different forms in their experience—complaints about call center cabs not being on time and the perceived inability to start a family started circling around an unspoken dark nucleus: night work.

One could try to understand the puzzled lack of resistance against night work as simply a matter of choice: these agents *chose* to work at night, right? They were not misled or forced into night work. Why should they resist what they chose themselves? This understanding of choice as freedom is not new. It could be applied with equal force to nineteenth-century factory work, which was after all wage labor, not slavery. Workers could always choose not to work in the factory in favor of unemployment, instead of striking and resisting the regime of long working hours. Don't these young college graduates, too, have a choice between a period of unemployment and the discomforts of night work at a call center?

It is at this point that we may begin to solve the puzzle about the lack of struggle in a novel way. The agent's choice exists only in the economic realm where one is expected to choose between financial well-being or its absence.

And agents are only being rational in making the choice. But economic well-being has unhinged from social and physical well-being in a way that an increase in well-being in one domain reduces it in another. While choices are being made in the economic realm, complaints are arising in the social and physical realms. Economic, social, and biological itineraries have diverged to such an extent that they seem in this case to be working at cross purposes, leaving no over-arching notion of well-being, no universal vantage point from which to launch a struggle. Call centers afford us a perfect place to look at the diverging paths—social, economic, physiological—of this ensemble of life.

## Social Well-Being

One Sunday afternoon I sat chatting with Vikas in the apartment that he shared with five other male agents packed into three bedrooms. The apartment was part of a less expensive complex, at least by Gurgaon standards, housed in an off-white five-story building in a quieter part of Gurgaon. The apartment reminded me vaguely of my days preparing for the civil services exam with friends in a college hostel in the late eighties. Given the unkempt character of the place, with more agents than bedrooms, it also gave hints of a "hacker hostel" in San Francisco. On second thought, though, the difference between those places and this was stark. In contrast to the intense social life and male camaraderie of a hostel, this place was empty; two agents were still sleeping in a separate bedroom while the other three had gone their separate ways to renew dwindling friendships and family life on a Sunday afternoon.

By this time Vikas had become a friend; he already knew that I was actually doing research while working at GoCom. As I began to record my conversation with him, he received a phone call from his father, who for the next twenty minutes appeared to berate him about his job. Vikas, on the defensive, kept repeating in Hindi that it was a temporary situation. After he hung up, I asked him what it was about.

"For the last two or three days he [father] has been asking why don't you go for an MBA or something like that . . . ," Vikas explained in English. "OK, for the time being this [job] is fine. Yeah, I'm earning money, but what will happen after some time? After two or three years?" His father's reasons for pressuring Vikas were twofold: first, he was worried that Vikas would run out of options in a few years, losing opportunities to find a more respected job. The second reason was marriage and family.

"There was once [this guy] working for a call center," Vikas recalled one of his friends who worked at a call center. "He was very happy; everything was going fine. But the moment he got married, he said, now [Vikas], I cannot work here. Otherwise you will spoil your life, your spouse's life and your family life will go to hell." Agents' experiences continuously hinted how the itineraries of night work and social life were at odds with each other.

Vikas seemed to have a debonair, carefree, nonchalant, and more or less uncaring demeanor. He was one of the few male agents who did not show interest in their female colleagues. But on close scrutiny, he turned out to be a man full of doubt, with unresolved personal conflicts, and he was deeply caring. Working with him at GoCom, I had already begun to notice the presentation of his self as a façade. Once I announced to my group that I could read palms and decipher people's character. People looked at me with disbelief. In India, as perhaps everywhere, such "knowledge" is quite welcome; I already had a few palms stretching out in front of me. This announcement certainly broke the ice, giving me my first opening into people's lives. I began by reading Vikas's hand. I had no knowledge of palmistry, of course. It was a playful deception that—I would later tell everyone—was just a game for fun. I started by telling him that he presents this persona of an uncaring, cool young man, and nothing could be further from the truth. I knew he came from Meerut, a small town in Uttar Pradesh. In Gurgaon where presumably there was less depth to friendships, Vikas portrayed himself to be even less caring than others, who presumably suffered from Simmelian blasé attitude of the metropolis. My first sentence took him by surprise, which everyone sitting around noticed. They all said they had never seen anyone so startled. On my further reading, Vikas agreed with me on many details about his personality that I was able to imagine, establishing me as the astrologer of the group.

By the time of this interview in his apartment, Vikas was ready to share all details of his life. He admitted his father was worried that if he got stuck in this position for long, he could not have a normal life, anxious about how Vikas could get married and start a family. I mentioned to him an agent who worked along with his girlfriend at GoCom, so it was theoretically possible to find someone who also worked at the same call center. But we both knew that it was not a common situation.

While Vikas could fend off his father's pressures for the foreseeable future, one could only imagine how female agents coped with family pressures. Marriage continues to haunt middle-class Indian women as a dominant family concern. Women, too, seemed as interested in marriage as in their career. At GoCom, all women in my group indicated in many conversations that call center work was not going to be their career. Their complaints against call center work always came in terms of family and social life. Nocturnal labor was at cross-purposes with the historical development of human sociality, family life, and child development. Night work was an already assumed problem, a problem they did not overtly talk about, knowing well it was unsolvable. After all, one couldn't change the time zone of the places they were serving. Solving the problem of night work in this case would only mean shutting down the call center.

Night work shaped those who would work at GoCom. Every agent whom I had come to know by this time at GoCom was single except Krishnan, who appeared to be in his late forties, and who also appeared to take his job more seriously than others. Mukul, on the other hand, joined GoCom precisely in order to avoid marriage. Call centers were a perfect choice for someone running away from family life. He migrated from a southern state where he worked as a foreign trade manager, earning about Rs. 18,000 to 20,000 a month, quite a bit higher than what he was earning now.

"They were signing me up to get married. I just wanted to get away from the family with long distance," Mukul replied nonchalantly to my query why he left a better job. After getting a normal daytime job, pressures for marriage rise dramatically in middle-class India. Mukul moved to Gurgaon chasing his girlfriend who he had first met in Chad. It was not too difficult for Mukul to start a new career at Gurgaon's call centers, allowing him to be near his girlfriend. There was one problem: She was married and lived with her husband in Gurgaon.

"Things changed. She got pregnant, not by me," Mukul confessed with a touch of sadness. "She got pregnant . . . her husband moved to Italy. She also moved on the second or third [of this month]." It was possible that she wanted to stop her relationship with him to save her marriage, but Mukul did not think so.

More immediate than marriage and family were concerns about social erasure through night work. In my conversations with agents, the topic of the night shift came up frequently but was seldom the target of direct concern. Tarun was one of the few who expressed this concern squarely by calling himself a "walking ghost."

"Hardly anybody recognizes you, nobody recognizes you," Tarun ruminated, "you go out when nobody sees you; you come in when nobody sees you. When you wake up in the evening, you see all your newspapers. At 8 PM, you pick up your newspapers when it's your good morning. You browse through the news for the day that happened yesterday . . . After a while you stop listening to the news; then you stop reading the newspapers. All you want to do is get your pillow and sleep; get up, go, make your calls, come back, and sleep. You don't want to know what's happening in the world."

Still, nights at GoCom had their own sociality. Our nightly life had its rhythms and schedules; we made friends, for instance, Vikas and I, who worked the same schedule. However, after the training period was over and we graduated to making real calls, everyone worked alone on the crowded floor. All the agents had their own headsets, their own computer monitors, their self-contained desk partitions, their separate sales goals, separate triumphs and disappointments. We could talk with each other only during the "lunch hour" every night. There were hardly any other breaks allowed by the dialer-paced work, not enough shared intervals for the social life at work to gain depth of its own. In a way this is no different from other professions where employees' performances are individually assessed, where they have to meet their own targets and frequently have to compete with each other to meet these. The difference lay in the temporal symmetry that daytime workers could enjoy with others, so their evening social life after work remained intact, relieving them from their dependence on workplace sociality. Agents' best friends still tended to be from their pre–call center world; the looming question was how long such friendships could endure without their presence or participation.

Once the loss of social life dawned on her, Ranjana decided to quit, a decision with which she was quite happy, as she noted about her batch mates: "I think sixteen of us quit, and two people are still there. We did not know [if we would leave] the day we met, but we all ended up leaving. So it was good. I think everybody who stays on in a call center does not have an option. That is what I feel. The day I quit, senior people who were working there for two years said they also want to quit, but they can't. I said, 'why?' and they said, 'Where will we get a job?'" They were correct. I realized there were three kinds of agents at GoCom. First, agents who came to work at a call center for the first time; second, agents who quit another call center for better pay at GoCom, and last, those who after having quit the industry, looked for, but failed to find, a daytime job, and thus decided to return. Vikas himself was one such agent: his neutral accent, his knowledge of American geography, work processes, or American customers were of no use in any other industry.

It was disappointing for him to realize that his skills and training were not so functional in the world of daytime jobs. There were a few domestic call centers but they were not as well paying in terms of salary and other perks. He could keep looking for regular daytime jobs, the prospects for which seemed bleak, or he could go back to the call center industry where finding a job again would not be a problem. He decided for the latter. This is how I met him at GoCom, and learned from him many effective—if not always fair—ways to make a sale.

To be fair, call centers did offer people who couldn't fit in the daytime world a space where all that mattered was their ability to talk. Tarun told me a story of a person who lost his leg in a motorbike accident. "So, one leg was amputated and the other one was very sensitive," Tarun recalled. "He took up this call center job, and that gave him a lot of self-respect. Because he was equally good. We don't have to run around in a call center; you have to just sit down and make calls. He used to come on his crutches, but he was a very good caller. One of the best performers in the center." Still, for the average agent, Tarun felt, night work was a burden: "He comes back; he has no social life. He is a dead man technically."

With a few exceptions like Tarun who openly recognized the burdens of night work, the practice itself remained beyond criticism for most agents. Yet, in numerous conversations, the problem of nocturnal labor raised concerns about its opposites: normal job, normal family life, marriage, children. But most vociferous criticism was directed against what was supposed to help one's transition into night work: cabs. Just as concerns about marriage and family substituted for complaints against night work, one of the perks of the job—the pickup and drop-off facility—came in for severe criticism, a facility that often added to the length and burden of nocturnal labor performed by a diurnal body.

## Physical Well-Being: Displaced Anger at Cabs

One area of direct concern was long hours of night work. Working for GoCom's telemarketing campaign for a British company, Mukul brought up the subject. When they were failing to meet their monthly target, he was putting in twelve hours a night, "Thursday, Friday, Saturday, Sunday." Although the UK-oriented shift had better hours than the one focused on the United States, he was being picked up at 3:30 PM, ending work at 12 AM and reaching home at 3:30 AM, and "the next day," Mukul noted, "the cab comes around 1 PM . . . Saturday and Sunday . . . And you can't ask the management why you are doing it or why we are not being paid for that." Typically, Mukul blamed the problem on GoCom, which he called a C-class call center. These call centers "just exploit employees so much. Because some of them [employees] just don't have any [other] chance [on the job market]. Maybe they are just working for one month or two months." Long hours of work whether during day or night appeared similar to him.

But the biggest indirect gripe against night work centered on the cabs, also regarded as one of the perks of working for international call centers. As GoCom leased hundreds of cabs for picking up the agents from their homes and dropping them off in the wee hours, this benefit itself was the biggest source of complaints among the agents. Being picked up by the company cab meant losing control of one's commute. I noticed that for many agents, depending on their location, the pickup time started an hour or two before their work hours, and they were often dropped off an hour or two after they completed their shift.

Being dropped off late was particularly hard, especially after a whole night of work when their nerves were frazzled and patience wore thin. Each cab picked up five to eight agents from various locations in Delhi and Gurgaon. While the cab driver's beat was well organized, agents often found themselves waiting for an hour or a half hour either to be picked up or dropped off.

"You know, this affects a human being so much, working in a C-class call center . . . After the logout time, it is half an hour just waiting for the cab; [and to be picked up] one day the cab comes at 1:30 PM to your house and the next day it comes at 2:30 PM . . . that one hour is just wasted for you." Mukul, as often, directed his complaints against GoCom. I reminded him that he lived in Gurgaon, only a fifteen-minute ride from work, so why he got picked up so early, an hour before the shift began. As he lived closer to work, he did not need to be dragged to far off places only to be brought back to work. Shouldn't he be one of the last ones to be picked up?

"Yeah, that is what I am saying," he replied, "my cab, see, right now what time the phone call came [the cab driver usually calls agents before picking them up]? It was at 2:56 [PM]. My shift is at 5:00 [today] . . . They pick up maybe six people, and take one and a half hours [to do that] . . . Normally for my shift the cab's moving time is at 2 o'clock. And 4:00–4:30 is the reporting time for the cab. So it's two hours when the cab comes for the first pickup at 2:30. Then, five or six pickups . . . sometimes I leave 3:30, sometimes I leave by 4:00. Sometimes, I have waited in Mega Mall from 2:30 to even 4:30–5:00. And there is no responsible person [to complain that] the cab is late . . . [also] I am staying inside . . . it's difficult for the cab to come there." Mukul had to go outside the complex and wait on the street by Mega Mall. The problem of cabs was not limited to GoCom.

"You know transport is one big problem. Each company has its problem, confusion with transport." Geeta who had worked in many call centers gave an example: "The problem was my shift gets us off five minutes earlier, so maximum 3:15 or 3:30 [A.M.] I am home. One day the lady, the manager, kept us in a meeting where we were not required . . . they were talking about the problem they were facing on the floor while taking calls. So that's not nice. You finish your work at 2:30, and then, you wait till, the next shift will finish at 4:30, the cab will leave at 5 o'clock. So you are hanging out, doing nothing in the middle of the night."

Managers complained that the cab service was such a nice perk, but they couldn't find an agent who did not complain about it. They remained mystified why agents complained so much about small lapses of the cab service. To me, however, the question was why they did not complain more, or why they did not see night work itself as a problem.

But let us acknowledge that the cabs of call centers did not necessarily provide a slow service. Indeed, they were a bit too fast in physical terms. Their speed was a concern not only for call centers but for Gurgaon in general. Given the fact that they were leased in the hundreds and thousands, their speed along with sheer number was a much-discussed media topic.

## Cabs, Speed, and Neutrality

As the nights of Gurgaon connected live with the days of overseas cities, call center taxis speeding to and from Delhi turned the streets into a strange global clash, as divergent timetables of London, New York, Seattle, and Sydney came together in Gurgaon. The combination of a strict call center schedule, mostly decided by the daytime hours, say, of the United States, and relatively less crowded nighttime streets of Gurgaon, made call center cabs lethally neutral to the world around them.

"Due to water-tight login times, cab drivers have to meet sharp deadlines every day," the Economic Times reported, "Cab drivers often over-speed to save on the penalty imposed by BPOs if they delay on reporting times" (ET 2007).

During my own commutes at night between Gurgaon and Delhi in 2005, I had an odd experience of extreme hurry in the middle of nocturnal calm, a war zone of rushing Toyota Qualises aggressively weaving around slower Tata trucks. The roads offered a visual feel for how global currents reframe the so-called local life, disconnecting it from itself. To use an analogy, the disconnect is similar to what is visible when individuals on mobile phones appear to be both present and absent, present to the party at the other end and absent to the immediate social space around them. Their functional connection to another space heralds a disconnection from their immediate location, separating the social and the physical. As they talk to the air on their hands-free mobile phones, they may give an appearance of lunacy to persons innocent of cellphone culture. Yet their behavior recalibrates the meaning of what is generally considered local and social space, or even public and private space. Granted, cellphone calls may be geared toward meeting someone in person at a physical location (but then it would be a physical meeting). Time spent on mobile calls and time spent in physical meetings remain analytically separate events. Arguably, call center cabs are also present and absent in the same way as they respond to calls from another world. Persons on the cellphone are prone to bumping into things around them or crashing their cars because of a clear disconnect between them and their surroundings. So are these taxis. The speed of call center taxis unmindful of their surroundings was a matter of concern in Delhi and Gurgaon (Vishnoi 2006). In 2007, a call center taxi mowed down seven people in Delhi, a widely reported event in the newspapers.

"Seeing the rash behaviour of call centre cab drivers," the *Economic Times* reported, "the Delhi Traffic Police came out with a notice threatening to cancel permits if cab drivers speed over 40 kph in Delhi limits." But the threat of permit cancellation was replaced by meditation. No, it's not a typographical error. "The BPO industry wants to initiate its notorious bunch of cab drivers into meditation to bring some sense of discipline into their driving," continued the *Economic Times*. "Even in the past there have been a spate of incidents of rash driving by BPO cabbies, which have caused fatal accidents. There's a thought within the BPO industry that cab drivers, who are often on duty almost 16 hours a day, have little time to catch up with sleep or family" (ET 2007).

If we consider sleep as physical or biological good, we can conceive of family as a social good; however, it is the economic good that is driving the driving behavior. In physical terms, the level of stress among cab drivers was a matter of concern. The president of the Call Centre Association of India, Sam Chopra, was reported as saying, "We are looking at yoga consultants and meditation sessions to reduce their stress levels. We are also devising tools for stress management, as a rash cab driver not only endangers his own life, but also that of the other seven people in the cab" (ET 2007). To help alleviate their stress levels, the industry was considering courses like Art of Living. Many vendors made drivers do double shifts stretching up to sixteen or seventeen hours, something that was considered dangerous for traffic safety.

But perhaps more crucial than the number of work hours were the hours of work. Night hours have important connections with accidents in general. Major disasters in recent memory occurred at night or early morning from fatigue-related human inattention: Valdez, Chernobyl, Bhopal, Three Mile Island, or the Rhine Chemical spill. One could add to the list more frequent automobile and trucking accidents to assess the consequences of neutrality toward the difference between day and night. Studies show an increased risk of road accidents driving home from a night shift (Gold et al. 1992; Ohayon et al. 2002; Stutts et al. 2003) and shift workers have a much higher rate of highway accidents compared to day workers (Akerstedt, Kecklund, and Horte 2005; Richardson, Miner, and Czeisler 1990; Smith, Folkard, and Poole 1994). Call center cabs drop off employees early in the morning, the hours associated with a five- to six-fold increase in the risk of having a highway accident of any kind, sleep-related (Horne and Reyner 1995) or not (Akerstedt et al. 2001). But the global techno-economy has not only managed to remain neutral to the day/night difference; its neutrality has grown in the global age. Instead of worker resistance or legal restrictions, we notice a gradual lifting of restrictions on night work around the world, further complicating the puzzle of widespread indifference to the graveyard shift.

To be fair, it is not accurate to suggest that there have been no restrictions on night work. After global victories against labor regimes of long hours, there did emerge a set of restrictions on night work, though, curiously, pertaining mostly to women worldwide. On the physical, but not economic, register, nocturnal labor was perceived as problematic, pressing against the age-old social dynamic of sex and gender, a dynamic that also eventually leads us to the question of physical well-being. But lately, these restrictions on night work are being lifted, allowing economic well-being, or rather market forces, to dominate the discussion.

## De-sexing the Night

India's call centers have been at the forefront of the push for lifting restrictions on the night shift. These restrictions have pertained mostly to women worldwide. Following the International Labour Organization's (ILO) convention 89, the Indian Factories Act of 1948 prohibited women from working at night as a safety measure, stating: "No women shall be required or allowed to work in any factory except between the hours of 6 A.M. and 7 P.M. (Section 64 [b], Factories Act of 1948)." As call centers are not considered manufacturing operations or factories, they operate under state-based Shops and Establishments Acts that tend to follow the Factories Act's prohibition on night work for women in most states. But in a changing climate, in April 2000 the governor of Tamil Nadu, followed by a few other states, exempted the software industries in the state from the chapter II provisions of the Tamil Nadu Shops and Establishments Act of 1947. Karnataka followed suit. In effect, the rule on opening and closing hours of the shop no longer applied to call centers and software firms.

In many states, call centers started employing women for night work before the law could be brought in line. In 2002, Delhi's call centers were warned by the *Financial Express*, "Call centre operators beware! If you are not following the provisions of the Delhi Shops and Establishments Act of 1954, or not seeking exemptions under it, you may be prosecuted. According to the provisions of the Act, women employees are not allowed to work overnight and also those working on holidays are entitled to double wages and compensatory leave" (FE 2002). However, call centers were not prosecuted, and exemptions were granted as a matter of routine. "Clearly, provisions of the various states' decades-old Acts that relate to holidays, the number of days offices must remain shut and working hours," another newspaper reported, "can't realistically be followed due to the exigencies of the new business environment" (Dugal 2008). The law itself needed to be changed. The Factories Act was sought to be brought in line with the global economic regime. The existing labor laws, partly a legacy of the socialist era since India's independence, were considered too protective of labor to be congruent with programs of liberalization. The Government of India appointed the Second National Commission on Labour in 2001 after a period of seventy-two years in order to consider the demands of global competitiveness, and "rationalize" the existing standards of labor protection while ensuring "a *minimum* level of protection and welfare to labour" (italics added). What is noteworthy about the legal shift is not necessarily a sudden social transformation or legal enlightenment but a crucial event of India's integration into the global economy.

In the meantime, the ILO also revised its prohibition contained in Convention 89 of 1948 in its Protocol of 1990 to the Night Work (Women) Convention, providing new exemptions from the prohibition of night work by leaving it to local representatives of the employers and workers to reach an agreement. The European Union took a step further when its Court of Justice issued a ruling in 1991, declaring the ILO Convention to be incompatible with the principle of the equality of the sexes proclaimed by community directive 76/207.

The pressure of global markets opened up by information and communicational technologies reframed night work both in India and the European Union as a matter of equal opportunity and women's freedom of work, instead of equal exploitation, making "freedom from" night work sound anachronistic.

"The Shops and Establishments Acts are well meaning, yes, but many of their provisions have lost relevance and become outdated over the decades," reported LiveMint, a business newspaper of the *Hindustan Times* group (Dugal 2008). Restrictions on night work seemed to have lost relevance, as if the human body transformed from being diurnal to nocturnal in those decades. The new discourse pushed the problems of night work below the threshold of perception. India was one of the first to ratify the ILO's revision of its convention 89. In contrast to a century of protests against long hours of work and corresponding labor regulations, the growing global relaxation of regulations against night work signaled an important global transformation that went almost unnoticed relative to its significance.

Yet nights do not become equal by a facile argument about the equality of sexes. The European Union, the ILO, and the Indian government all provided extra safeguards for the occupational safety of women. The ILO continued its prohibition on night work for "women workers during a period before and after childbirth of at least 16 weeks, of which at least eight weeks shall be before the expected date of childbirth," a difference toward which the ILO could not allow neutrality. After all, the work of reproduction was still carried out only by women. In India, the Factories (Amendment) Bill of 2005, too, declared additional safeguards for women's "dignity, honour and safety and their transportation from the factory premises to the nearest point of their residence." The clause on transportation was an implicit recognition of different implications of night work for men and women as factories and offices could not be isolated from their surroundings. One of the reasons why Gurgaon's call centers developed the practice of picking up and dropping off their employees was the need to provide protection against unequal nights and male aggression outside the premises. Other reasons include practical benefits of getting employees to work on time during the sketchy hours of public transportation.

Let us admit that the lifting of restrictions on women's right to work at night does have a positive ring of gender neutrality in matters of employment. Why shouldn't a woman be able to work at night if she so chooses? Perhaps the notion of gender neutrality requires more thought. The idea often provokes two incompatible, though understandable, positions. While the first condemns neutrality, the second celebrates it against practices of discrimination. From the first position gender neutrality allows the employer to ignore important gender differences. For instance, motherhood is widely regarded as a disadvantage in the labor market. In the name of equal employment, gender neutrality may end up discriminating against one gender more than the other. Paradoxically, on the other hand, neutrality is also a celebrated political stand against bias and discrimination of various kinds. From gender neutrality to calls for a color-blind society, to recent campaigns for net neutrality, the idea of being neutral to difference is favored, especially when the situation pertains to discrimination against differences based on color, sex, sexual orientation, or ethnicity.

The above paradox is the basis of a historical dilemma between neutrality and difference. In the first half of the twentieth century, the issue of special protective legislation for women created a split within the global women's movement, as discussed by Elisabeth Prügl (1999) in the context of homework. While equal-rights feminists condemned the legislation for its discriminatory effects, union women defended it, arguing that women's working conditions were at times objectively different from those of men. In the late 1920s this led to a split of the International Alliance of Women (IAW). Equal rights feminists, on the other hand, defined women as free and equal individuals in the liberal sense, disregarding motherhood as well as any associations of apparent weakness and dependence with womanhood.

Theories of difference have since become more sophisticated. Feminist studies of science present strong arguments against the language of neutrality (Butler 1990; Harding 1992). I identify this kind of feminist scholarship as an argument for what I call the politics of hierarchy-free difference, not a normative stance that tends to promote a unified approach but a critical stance against any pretense of overcoming difference through a universal ideal. It is no surprise that this approach finds partial and standpoint perspectives (Smith 1987) more effective, for they avoid the "god-trick of seeing everything from nowhere" (Haraway 1991). By bringing out the embodied nature of vision, for instance, Haraway proposes a doctrine of embodied objectivity against the false transcendence of all limits and responsibility: "The moral is simple: only partial perspective promises objective vision." Haraway specifies "embodied vision" further by a simple example of walking with her dog and "wondering how the world looks without a fovea and very few retinal cells for colour vision, but with a huge neural processing and sensory area for smells . . . The 'eyes' made available in modern technological sciences shatter any idea of passive vision . . . all eyes, including our own organic ones, are active perceptual systems, building in translations and specific ways of seeing, that is, ways of life" (Haraway 1991, 190).

One's experience is bound up with one's location. So sexual differences matter, but no hierarchy can be established between sexes. There is no universal vantage point against which one can create a hierarchical order, no metacode to subjugate difference. Dogs' sense of smell and human sense of smell cannot be compared normatively because no common norms can be developed; we can never experience what it is like to be a dog smelling the sidewalk brush. We can always reconstruct the dog's sense of smell through some scientific means, but then they will be scientific, not canine, constructions.

Haraway, above, echoes Niklas Luhmann (1984), who theorized all knowledge as system-specific knowledge, denying any possibility of universal, transcendental knowledge independent of the particular system of observation. Thus, the problem with scientific or economic systems is not only their neutrality to differences important in other realms but also their claim to universality, the enforcement of their perspective as the sole authority on human condition, devaluing experiences arising from differences that fail to register as important for economic or scientific concerns.

At this point, let me offer a simple, if limited, definition of neutrality: Neutrality is *indifference to difference*. When a system of observation interprets a possible signal from another domain as noise, it is being neutral to that domain, reducing potential complexity in its construction of reality. Economic theory, for instance, is largely neutral to a day and night difference, a difference that is registered as crucial in chronobiology. Let us admit that neutrality is often useful for reducing complexity in observations. Scientific findings treat differences in the religious realm as irrelevant to its enterprise, often for good reasons. While Newton's belief in God may have kept him wedded to the notion of absolute space whose eternal and infinite existence was secured through God's omnipresence (Newton 2004), all sciences have turned a deaf ear to theology over the years. A scientist may entertain religious beliefs but she cannot publish a scientific paper using a religious argument. Religion may put an external pressure on scientific practice (e.g., debates on cloning) but not on scientific method. This indifference may have consequences, as the scientific functionalization of life may initiate a gradual loss of life's meaning and myths, something crucial to psychic and social realms.

It is in this context that we may revisit the question of night neutrality and the apparent gender-neutral space of India's call centers (Mirchandani 2005) and frame it as part of the growing neutrality of the global techno-economic system to social and cultural differences. This neutrality, mostly technical, legal, and economic in construction, tends to discount and thus flatten the felt differences of social, cultural, and even bodily rhythms. Yet the growing indifference is hardly neutral in its function and effects, as I discuss shortly.

## Biological Well-Being: Male-Female and Diurnal-Nocturnal Differences

Working for GoCom I experienced firsthand how night work affected the daily life of an agent. On the social plane, I had to give up evening and weekend get-togethers with my old college friends working in New Delhi at the time. Many of them complained about my sudden disappearance, but once they came to know of my adventures at GoCom, they understood, of course. I also had to give up any semblance of family life. When I reached home in the wee hours, my wife and three-year-old son were asleep; they woke up and went about their day while I slept. By midafternoon, I had already left before my wife could get our son from a daycare school, which was a good half hour away. I realized I had to change the situation to maintain sanity. Instead of taking the call center cab, which would add—agents were right—two extra hours to my commute from South Delhi to Gurgaon each day, I began to use my brother's car. Fortunately, my brother had just bought a new car, and I could borrow his old car for my nightly commutes. This allowed me to stay in Delhi until late afternoon, see my son after his school, and then drive to Gurgaon.

But driving had its own perils. It must have been five in the morning on my way back after the night shift once, I hit a stray dog and killed him. The road was dark but clear, no fog, except perhaps in the head. I saw the young dog trying to cross the road and made the decision to keep going, thinking by the time I reached the spot he would have crossed the road. Seeing the car, the dog decided to go back, something I didn't notice. He met his fate right in the middle of the road. The car's radiator started leaking, and I rushed home before it was too late. The experience of hitting a soft, furry, heavy mass of life with hard steel remains etched in my mind. It was only after doing some research on sleep deprivation and nighttime accidents that I realized that my decision to keep going while the dog was trying to cross the road was an unfortunate nocturnal decision made by a diurnal creature. This brings me to the topic of physical well-being seen through the lens of the biological sciences, which, unlike economics, do distinguish between day and night hours of work. Personally, I remember not seeing the sun for days on end, often going out of the apartment to catch the last rays of the afternoon sun just before the commute. I also remember having a constant feeling of jet lag, a mix of sleep deprivation and disengagement with the world around.

"I can't take it," Geeta voiced my concerns. "Number one, as I told you, in the day I can't sleep properly. Then, so much of that coffee, smoking . . . Coffee, ginger tea, elaichee tea; we also have these counters, GE has Barista [coffee shop] but basically it's the heavy food, and sedentary job, just sitting." Geeta was slightly overweight and seemed aware of night work's effects without perhaps knowing that science, too, has found a convincing association between sleep deprivation and weight gain (Patel et al. 2006; Harvard 2013).

Here we may want to revisit the question of long hours of work versus wrong hours of work. Are long hours of work that prompted a century of protests more burdensome than night work? The biological sciences would argue otherwise. The burden of night and shift work, according to neurobiology, may be greater on the body than long hours of day work. Let us first remind ourselves how we are connected to, indeed constructed by, the planet's spin and movement.

Sleep is part of biological rhythms, ranging from cycles lasting one per millisecond to those lasting one per several years, beating in a single cell or pulsing through the whole body. Some of these rhythms are part of our daily experience: breathing, heart rate, ovarian and sleep cycles. Kidneys slow down at night, and the liver works slowest in the morning. All these rhythms are seen in biology as working together in a dance ensemble to constitute life. Sleep itself is part of circadian rhythms, whose disruption affects circulatory, respiratory, and other functions. It is important to note that the central circadian, that is, twenty-four-hour, clock that regulates the timing of sleep and wake cycle in mammals is endogamous. It is internal to the body and thus independent from day-night cycles outside. Neurobiology claims to have found its exact location: a small region of the hypothalamus—the suprachiasmatic nucleus (SCN) (Aschoff 1981). Yet the functioning of the internal clock is not neutral to the earth's rotation on its axis. They appear deeply choreographed.

To ascertain the circadian clock's independence, a golden hamster was maintained in constant darkness for 100 days while a computer recorded his wheel-running activity. His activity rhythm showed remarkable precision under free-running conditions devoid of any timing cues. In total darkness, the hamster with no clue about day or night was active during the day and inactive at night. However, the experiment also revealed that the onset of activity showed a period slightly greater than twenty-four hours throughout the 100 days (also, a gradual decline in activity per day due to the decrease in testicular size and serum testosterone levels due to exposure to constant darkness) (Turek and Zee 1999). That is, the hamster's circadian rhythms, being slightly more than twenty-four hours, lost touch with the external world over time. The fact that circadian rhythms do not exactly match the period of the rotation of the earth on its axis demands that the outside world of twenty-four-hour, light and dark (LD) cycle must somehow choreograph, synchronize, or *entrain* the internal clock system regulating circadian rhythms. The day and night cycle is clearly the major entraining agent of circadian rhythms, allowing the period of circadian rhythms to match the period of the LD cycle.

Here one can argue that if the circadian clock—a timekeeping, temperature-swinging, enzyme-controlling device—is internal, we can simply forgo the entraining by the LD cycle, using nightly work hours for the purpose, instead. Even if the sleep-wake cycle is normally timed to occur at a specific phase relative to the external cycle of light-dark exposure, a person can make sure to get the same amount of sleep to maintain sleep homeostasis* but let go of LD exposure by using a simple alarm clock alongside his or her internal circadian rhythms for sleep-wake cycles, and forget about waking up to sunlight.

But it turns out that major sleep episodes are relatively deficient when they occur at the wrong time of day. The circadian rhythms of shift workers do not

---

*Sleep deficit elicits a compensatory increase in the intensity and duration of sleep.

usually phase shift to adapt to working at night and sleeping during the day, resulting in poor performance and reduced alertness during night work and poor daytime sleep at home (Burgess, Sharkey, and Eastman 2002). Recent data imply that while circadian (sleep-wake cycle) and homeostatic processes (sleep debt compensation) are separate processes, they are closely integrated at the molecular level (Franken and Dijk 2009). Time of day regulates subcellular trafficking in mammalian brain (Gerstner et al. 2012), and the sleep deprivation–induced restorative, slow wave sleep attains higher levels when recovery sleep starts at dark onset (Curie et al. 2013).

Clearly, chronobiology is not neutral, by definition, to the diurnal-nocturnal difference, to the temporality of the hormonal realm. It constructs a different understanding of work where one work hour is not the same as another. But what happens if we defy these processes? Aren't humans, unlike all other species, often awake when their internal biological clock is telling them it is time to sleep, and often trying to sleep when the circadian clock is shooting signals throughout the brain and body that it is time to be awake? It is routine for humans to cognitively override their internal circadian clock so their sleep-wake timing can be scheduled to meet the personal demands of their social and work schedule (Turek and Zee 1999). It appears that night and shift work takes this human habit to an extreme where the functional choreography of sleep rhythms, eating rhythms, and solar rhythms comes undone. The new functional ensemble of the market, work, and personal goals makes previous assemblages dysfunctional with biological consequences.

Studies show how women's bodies register the dysfunctional effects—the alarm clock dissonance—of night work differently. For instance, hospital nurses engaged in shift work have been found to have irregular menstruation (Miyauchi, Nanjo, and Otsuka 1992). Other studies suggest that night work is associated with breast cancer risk among women (Davis et al. 2012; Megdal et al. 2005). In general, light exposure during night work suppresses the production of melatonin, a hormone connected with the system that regulates sleep-wake cycles. In addition to synchronizing the biological clock, melatonin is a potent, free radical scavenger and wide spectrum antioxidant, displaying significant anticarcinogenic action (Schernhammer et al. 2001; Tan et al. 1993), and its suppression during night and shift work, many studies find, leads to various cancer risks: breast, colorectal, endometrial (Hansen 2001; Schernhammer et al. 2003; Viswanathan, Hankinson, and Schernhammer 2007).

The significance of these studies may be judged by the fact that the International Agency for Research on Cancer (IARC) has classified shift work itself as a carcinogen (Straif et al. 2007). Night and shift work is found to affect pregnant women in yet another way. Female night workers have been found to be more vulnerable than male workers due to a number of adverse reproductive outcomes, such as spontaneous abortion, premature delivery, and low birth weight, which are shown to be related to night work (Costa 1997; Nurminen 1998; Scott and LaDou 1989). Fixed night work during pregnancy, more than shift work, is associated with late fetal loss (Zhu et al. 2004). A study found gendered differences in the way disrupted circadian homeostasis of sympathetic signaling promotes tumor development in mice. Irradiated and jet-lagged male wild-type mice show relatively lower tumor incidences and later onset of tumors than their female littermates. But the study did not find a significant gender-dependent difference in the time between tumor onset and total tumor incidence among irradiated and jet-lagged circadian gene-mutant mice (Lee et al. 2010).

While we must acknowledge that night and shift work may have gendered effects, we must also know that it adversely affects all diurnal creatures irrespective of their sex. If night and shift work could lead to breast cancer in women, it may lead to prostate cancer among men (Kubo et al. 2006). And for both genders, a Vitamin D–producing exposure to midday sun and ultraviolet radiation of specific low wavelength, 290–315 nm (UVB) is not available to nocturnal agents. Their evening commute does expose them to evening sunlight, which has a potential to cause skin cancers, as the error-checking apparatus for DNA inside skin cells operates most slowly in the early evening, allowing errors in our DNA to accumulate with greater possibility for cancer-causing mutations (Mitra 2011). A study hazards a guess that electric light may stimulate cancer development in children (Stevens 2012).

In short, the economic function of night work may lead directly to biological dysfunction. As call centers expand the global economy by functionally connecting previously secluded pockets of the world, they also produce dysfunctions in the biological realm. Recent biological understandings suggest that spatial, temporal, and seasonal differences are not external but embodied. The capitalist leveling of such differences is a flattening of the body's internal rhythms (Birth 2007). From daily circadian rhythms, including circadian clock correction through light and dark cycles of the day, to seasonal influences, for example, of diurnal rhythms in the onset of the plasma luteinizing hormone surge in pre-ovulatory women (Testart, Frydman, and Roger 1982), differences pertaining to the body's location on earth, its sex, and its age are material differences. Yet the economic discourse remains neutral to the consequences of night work registered differently in different bodies, consigning them to the sphere of externalities.

## No Universal Solution

Evidently, economic neutrality is not a mere passive event, signifying a lack of discrimination between sexes or between day and night. It is also an active imposition of neutrality in realms where those differences have material and experiential consequences. Nocturnal burdens imposed by capital on the diurnal body hinder biological self-regulation, which leads cells, tissues, bones, and muscle from below to refuse on account of their own laws and limits the dictates of capital from above, a refusal available in the shape of cancers, fetal loss, spontaneous abortion, premature delivery, and low birth weight mentioned earlier. The history of human suffering, Negt and Kluge (Langston 2013) point out, is a history of embattled self-regulations.

While the dominance and dysfunctions of economic functionalism are visible from social to biological realms, there are specific solutions emerging from different domains. The biological sciences can respond to the problem of night work only from their own functional realm. Their response tends to lie in the realm of medication. With pervasive sleep disorders plaguing the twenty-four hour global economy, biomedical systems have come up with extensive pharmacological solutions to mitigate the effects of work hours and work anxiety. But the biomedical sphere is capable of proposing solutions only from within its code of operation (e.g., it cannot propose a political solution), so it produced in the United States alone 43 million prescriptions in 2005, including drugs like Ambien (zolpidem), Sonata (zaleplon), Lunesta (eszopiclone), Dalmane (flurazepam), Restoril (temazepam), and ProSom (estazolam), to which one can add a larger sale of over-the-counter drugs.

In addition to general pharmacological responses, there have also been specific studies to see how the efficacy of the night shift can be enhanced. Experiments have been conducted to show that caffeine taken in precise doses and at precise times—for instance, 4 mg/kg of caffeine in two equal doses at two different times (10:30 P.M. and 1:20 A.M.)—can reduce the worker's sleepiness and performance impairment during night hours. As biological sciences gain greater understanding of the body's circadian, ultradian, and diurnal cycles, one of their solutions includes exposing night workers to bright light—from 7,000 to 12,000 lux—all along their night shifts and to darkness during daytime, utilizing the circadian phase-shifting effects of bright light (Burgess, Sharkey, and Eastman 2002; Richardson, Miner, and Czeisler 1990).

It is curious to note that the discoveries of chronobiology, in theory, are opposed to an economic system that disregards day and night differences; yet such discoveries end up being employed in the service of capital, which speeds up its transaction through biomedical solutions to sleep-related externalities. Clearly, biological research is often funded not for emancipation but for drug development, and most biological research both in its funding and function seems to enjoy a structural coupling with capitalism. With strategies for overcoming the body's nighttime fatigue and medications for sleep disorders solving the problem at the individual level, biological research has had the ironic effect of obscuring the conditions that produce sleep disorders. This does not mean that its discoveries cannot be appropriated for social purposes but it does explain why biological knowledge and the resulting pharmacological solutions have perhaps nipped in the bud possible forms of opposition to night work. There is no social movement against night work that could be compared with labor struggles for an eight-hour workday in the industrial age.

Psychology and cognitive sciences have proposed their own solutions. Techniques that have already been used to enhance the athlete's performance have been recommended for shift workers. Conducting an experiment, researchers found that if workers heard that the task would be "short and challenging," they showed fewer signs of vigilance loss than "monotonous and boring task expectancies" (Ware and Baker 1977). Variety in work tasks is as important as another technique—short rest breaks— which was also found to enhance alertness. Lille and Andlauer (1981) argue that activities should be renewed every 90 to 120 minutes to keep a sufficient alertness level. In vigilance research, it has been demonstrated that rest pauses help in maintaining efficiency (Bonnefond et al. 2004). A break at night has a beneficial effect on the fulfillment of tasks, if it lasts long enough (at least 20 minutes) and if it is accompanied with a real physical and mental break with the main activity, providing an individual or collective recreational leisure break (playing video games or doing motor activities) (Lancry and Stoklosa 1995). All call centers offer 30-minute lunch breaks in the middle of the night. Like biomedical responses, cognitive solutions to the problem may have a chilling effect on any social challenge to the legitimacy of night work.

Then we have the media sphere with its own solutions of raising awareness among, and providing information to, the public. *Femina*, a high-profile women's magazine in India, informs its readership that weight problems are more likely to occur at night than during regular shifts and that digestive processes slow down at night while Gurgaon's international call centers serve oily or fast food to their workers. The magazine suggests that call center employees should carry their own food consisting of fresh fruits and vegetables and do some weight training by lifting a one-liter bottle filled with water at work (*Femina* 2005). It also advises not to rotate shifts or jump from Australian to American to British processes, which have slightly different hours of work at night. While none of these solutions can ever bring back the choreography of sunlight, it is clear that they seek to pacify the conflict lodged in the heart of the global economy by providing individualized solutions for dealing with its adverse consequences—work-time inequality, fragmented families, sleep disorders, and other health consequences.

### Resolving the Puzzle

To resolve the puzzle with which this chapter began I reiterate the provocative answer: there is no single laboring body left for which to wage an eight-hour-day-like struggle. It has been mapped out differently with varying solutions depending on how different spheres—the market, biological sciences, mass media, cognitive science, and sociology—constitute reality and construct representations of laboring bodies (Fujimura 1996; Haraway 1997). For economics, a laboring body is a bloodless rational mind that makes choices, including the one about joining the call center. Here the problem of night work is not a problem in itself; indeed, it is an opportunity for a capitalist economy to multiply its transactions.

For biology, the laboring body is a breathing, heaving mass of rhythms; virtually all its parts—cells, tissues, and organs—are set to the cycles of day and night and seasons. Its internal clocks bind it not only to other creatures, but also to the spinning of the earth and rotation of the moon whose backbeat pulsates inside the chemistry of its cells. Written within the body, the biologist claims, is the birth of the solar system and workings of the planet itself (Shubin 2013).

For sociology, the laboring body is inherently social, connected not only to coworkers but also to family and friends who provide meaning to labor and its rewards. If one were given a hypothetical, extreme choice between a life of colossal wealth on an island without another human being in sight and a life of penury in an imperfect society, one would choose penury over wealth (e.g., the film *Castaway* shows how one becomes suicidal outside society). Night and shift work often puts workers out of synchrony with family, friends, and the daytime social world, producing a temporal asymmetry that is isolating. The daytime social life loses its relevance for nocturnal working life when one fields 250–300 calls a night.

It is important to remember that night work in itself is not exclusive to India's call centers. It is global and endemic. Night work haunts America with equal intensity. In the face of "mounting evidence that people who get too little sleep have a higher risk of weight gain and obesity than people who get seven to eight hours of sleep a night," Harvard School of Public Health reports, ". . . in 1998, 35 percent of American adults were getting 8 hours of sleep a night, and by 2005 that had dropped to 26 percent" (Harvard 2013). In social terms, recent research on pervasive nonstandard work schedules has uncovered a silent, swift, and invisible social fragmentation that besets America (Presser 2003). India's call centers demonstrate that the twenty-four-hour economy has become a global phenomenon. More important, for my argument, they demonstrate how various social spheres—work, consumption, knowledge—have attained such a high degree of functional isolation that for human experience they appear to have become dysfunctional together.

In all the preceding pages I have used the language of neutrality and indifference, instead of the more common and readily understood term—*alienation*—to highlight the problems of global labor and social life. But, isn't call center work a perfect example of alienated labor? As the agents perform dialer-paced work at night in an alien language and culture, following alien laws and time, aren't they experiencing estrangement from their work, culture, work process, and product and engaging in anything but "free conscious activity" proposed by Marx as the touchstone for unalienated labor?

Let me point out several reasons for my hesitation in using the term *alienation* or passing judgment on call center work. First, I have attempted a nonnormative analysis with a nonprescriptive ethic. One of the major points of this book is to point out divergent tracks of global life where independent prescriptions from different spheres preclude any universal, all-inclusive norm for unalienated labor. Let me be clear I am not using "universal norm" as a transhistorical absolute. I use it only in the limited sense of Habermasian consensus, whereby even scientific truths are not eternal but limited to historical periods of scientific consensus (otherwise, science would never be able to destroy its past understandings). Even in this limited sense, I do not see a normative consensus between autonomous discourses of different realms.

Of course, the biased social scientist in me sees the social prescription against night work as a universal solution: a prohibition on all night work on a global scale. For the sociologist, what is important is not more research on the fact that humans are diurnal animals whose circadian clocks need correction by the sun but a social movement against night work quite like industrial struggles for an eight-hour workday, a form of resistance against the consuming grip of the economic system on everyday social experience. But a social movement is by nature collective, not individual, action, and thus a highly contingent event. Although it is an improbable solution in the absence of a global regulatory regime, the sociologist can only hope for the crystallization of a global social movement against the practice of night work, barring essential, life-saving nighttime services (e.g., medical services). Such a movement can demand and put pressure on governments for a ban on night work as a human rights issue. One way to recover this possibility would be to hope for an unforeseen connection with the global environmental movement because limits on the nocturnal economy would at once be limits on energy use. Celebrating Earth Day every day, one could dream, may force change. But I doubt there will be universal agreement on this issue. Second, night work is only one aspect of call center work, which includes many other forms of putative alienation, pertaining to language, culture, and divergent norms of engagement.

My resolute attempt to stay away from offering a universal criterion for emancipation makes my argument susceptible to an intellectual paralysis. If I deny the possibility of universal, transcendental knowledge independent of particular discourses and systems of observation, I am stuck, it seems, with a hidden agenda of emancipation without the ability to specify norms of emancipation. By agreeing to the autonomy of multiplying discourses of economics, sociology, chronobiology, or law, I may have forfeited the right to criticize the practice from a clear vantage point.

Take the problem of night work in chapter 5, for example, where I argue that there is no single laboring body left for which a collective struggle can be waged. It has splintered across many domains and its cares and concerns have been divided up into the sociologist's concern for social well-being, the economist's concern for economic well-being, and the natural scientist's concern for physical well-being. While night work offers employment with obvious economic well-being, it also indicates a simultaneous isolation from the regular daytime social life and a fragmentation of family life when it is difficult to be together with one's spouse and children, reducing their social well-being. For a natural scientist, night work reduces well-being but for very different reasons, as it comes into conflict with the body's circadian rhythms and its diurnal frame, which is organized around light-dark cycles. Thus, nocturnal labor in call centers emerges as simultaneously good (economic well-being) and bad (social and biological well-being).

Is it possible, then, to provide a critique without basing it on a universal measure? This indeed has been my effort throughout this book, irrespective of its success: to put together a rudimentary critique not on the basis of an external, supposedly universal, norm according to which we could judge whether or not a practice is alienated labor but on the basis of the incoherence between different functional realms. We may call it an immanent critique of functionalism by showing how particular functional developments are simultaneously dysfunctional as a whole. Granted, the world has gone zealously functional, and all values and rewards seem to accrue within those realms of function; one's capability to do good science is lauded from within the norms and values of scientific enterprise. Breakthroughs in stem cell research are allowed to be judged not by Catholic values but only by scientific value. In the absence of overarching values common to different spheres, it makes sense to provide a critique of functionalization by highlighting its dysfunctions. I attempted to capture the paradoxical, dysfunctional effects of functionalization through the metaphor of alarm clock dissonance whether in biological or social domains. Functional developments appear to produce dysfunctions by their own internal criteria while conceptualizing society as a functional system. If we agree that the world society now differentiates along functional lines, then we must also pay heed to its dysfunctions, and try to understand its malignant tendencies.

I hope to have shown how the functional neutrality to differences in other realms produces dysfunctional effects. It is not a bleak assessment of call centers; rather, I use their sites, sounds, and selections to raise larger questions about the functionalization of life that attains a dysfunctional whole. I attempt to bring out how various attempts at functionalizing our world will necessarily be incomplete. There will always be implicit and explicit conflicts among different functional domains, producing dysfunctional effects. Thus, the economic understanding of night as just another period of productive activity clashes with the biological understanding of nocturnal period as well as the sociological understanding of social life, a conflict that does not remain abstract but enters into the personal lives of call center workers, in their conscious perceptions and unconscious experiences of the body.

## Difference and Indifference

Neutrality or indifference, let us be clear, is a necessity in certain circumstances. Isn't our conscious mind happily indifferent to all the goings-on in the kidney or the circulating blood in our veins? We become conscious only when there is trouble brewing in the body, often through the feeling of pain or uneasiness. All other workings of the body are ignored by consciousness. In the social realm, Georg Simmel characterized a big city dweller's indifference as a coping mechanism against nervous overstimulation, a way to negotiate the intensely crowded and fast-moving life of a metropolis, producing a blasé attitude (Simmel 1903). All knowing systems—from physics to physical eyes—must discard much of the overwhelming jingle and jangle of the world around in order to carve and construct their peculiar reality. They must be neutral and indifferent to some vibrations from the external world to build something specific for themselves. We may call this the primary logic of indifference.

Yet when indifference starts triggering alarm clock shocks or the blasé attitude as perpetual effects it threatens to collapse into dysfunction. We are wise enough to know that it is in the attention to difference that life exists. Sensitivity to environmental differences, quite like the peculiar construction of colors by human eyes, is how the knowing body flourishes and survives. Everyday social life also casts indifference as a negative attitude, and for good reasons. Neutrality to the plight of those in trouble, the less fortunate, or victims of violence diminishes social good.

The problem of developing difference-blind universal norms is precisely their supposed neutrality, which, as pointed out in chapter 5, often conceals not-so-neutral power relations. Universal norms are exclusionary if they require the neutrality toward particular standpoints in order to establish a common, general point of view. This form of neutrality becomes particularly offensive once universality is exposed as a myth concealing the majority's norms and conventions. The call to transcend difference often ends up imposing the majority perspective on minorities. Putative norms of equality, for instance, may produce more inequality rather than less since the presumed neutrality of difference-blind institutions often privileges the needs, interests, and identities of the majority group. This bias burdens minorities with specific demands or excludes them altogether, resulting in more inequality. For instance, standardized airbags in cars may save lives but they may structurally exclude children and women who tend to be shorter than the average height covered by the design (Jain 2006).

In step with difference-based feminism (Butler 1990; Haraway 1991; Smith 1987) and difference-based theories in general (Alexander and Colomy 1990; Deleuze 1994; Luhmann 1984; Wittgenstein 1953), I am acutely aware that differences are constituted by knowing systems, including feminism. Even a marked difference between man and woman is not a "natural" distinction existing outside all observation. Modes in which a body, consciousness, or sociology registers differences as sexual do not overlap, as each must constitute its world in its own languages. There is no sexual identity prior to a knowing body or a knowing discourse. By difference, therefore, I do not mean diversity. Difference is not a difference between preexisting self-identical objects (Deleuze 1994), for example, difference between male and female. The difference gets made in the very process of construction, observation, and drawing distinctions. There are no final, premade distinctions prior to constructions. There is no self-identical world out there to be discovered.

There are no immutable "brute facts," erroneously imagined by John Searle, on which socially constructed reality is temporally, ontologically, and logically dependent (Searle 1995). For Searle, social constructions—like language—are epistemologically, not ontologically, objective. Similarly, Ian Hacking (1999) claims that it is the ideas, not the objects to which the ideas correspond, that are socially constructed. Only when ideas, Hacking maintains, start interacting with, and affecting, people who move in the world of objects, can there be an indirect social construction of both objects and people that may be labeled "interactive kinds." Thus, "woman refugee" is constructed but "quarks" are not. "Quarks are not aware that they are quarks and are not altered simply by being classified as quarks" (Hacking 1999). Quarks, Hacking informs us, belong to an "indifferent kind."

Even steadfast social constructivists such as Berger and Luckmann (1990) have fallen for this argument, readily agreeing that biology precedes the social: "the necessity for social order as such stems from man's biological equipment," implicitly agreeing with a hierarchical model of reality, according to which some objects are ontologically or brutally real while others are socially constructed. Thus, pseudoscientific realism raises its head, stubborn and unrepentant, in the middle of constructionist doctrines. But, with apologies to Hegel, constructions are real and the real is constructed.

Is it possible to undo the divide between the real and constructed without falling into philosophical idealism? Let us try! Granted, there is an environment, a world without which no observation is possible, but this world is unknowable in its own language because the world does not have a language of its own (Putnam 1995). And the statement that our knowledge of the world somehow corresponds with the world is at best an inference and at worst a belief. There is no way to confirm it. To know if it corresponds with the world is to know the world in its own terms, which is, again, an absurd proposition. The basic premise here is Kantian but without his subject-centered transcendental idealism, which assumes the existence of individual mind as the condition of all understanding, a mechanism that transforms noumena into phenomena, or environmental stimulations into meaningful experiences. There are only different systems of construction without any hierarchy. Their corresponding constructions cannot be labeled as more or less real because there is no universal scale that can compare objects constructed by an organism, for instance, with objects created by language. There is no metalanguage that can compare the reality of refugee constructed within a system of nation-states with that of quarks in models of physics. Let us recall the Copenhagen Interpretation of quantum mechanics, as pronounced by Niels Bohr in 1927, that reality at the quantum scale cannot be taken to exist independently of the act of measurement. Because if this reality exists, what does it exist as? All reality prior to measurements, or sensory experiences, probably exists in a way that is not accessible, and must be transformed for understanding by measurements or sensory instruments of the body.

So it is too limiting to think of constructions in social terms alone. The physical world, as seen, heard, touched, and smelled by the body, is also a construction, though not of the social kind. When we touch another person, the experience of tactile solidity is a peculiar reality, constructed by physics in terms of intermolecular forces between atoms, and felt by the body as something solid. Thus, constructions of a sensory world by the body are of an entirely different order than the world constructed by physics.

Let us focus on light for a moment. The way human eyes discern, or construct, light relates to a functional accomplishment of making things visible and thus differentiating, for instance, between friendly and dangerous things; for example, between plants and snakes, or clear and obstructed paths. However, in the world of physics, visibility is not a defining factor of light, which, as electromagnetic radiation, includes a world invisible to the human eye. The visible spectrum is a tiny part of the electromagnetic spectrum, which ranges from gamma rays, X-rays, and microwaves to radio waves. Yet, the visible spectrum is where the human eye creates its magical, colorful world whose beauty is not relevant to the realm of abstract frequencies in physics. Each is a rigorous construction but not by the other's standards.

Here rigorous and ever-exacting measures of science should not be translated as certainty or a realistic image of the world. All sciences have grown by destroying their previous understandings, representative images, and old certitudes. Rigor is not perpetual certitude.

While constructions are internal to the system, which may be discursive like biology or nondiscursive like human eyes, and there is no possibility of a transcendental, overarching, or privileged realm of observation true to all spheres, we also realize that their workings are choreographed. The eye discerns color, the brain recognizes it, the language signifies it, and the poet writes about it. The problem seems to emerge when the choreography of self-regulated domains breaks down. In the case of call centers, the silent violence of night work is acutely felt by the body owing to reduced delta sleep, a kind of violence that may find indirect expression in accidents and cancers. Its violence is also felt in the social domain where it appears to put agents out of tune with the daytime social world. Only in the economic domain, night work is rewarded with income. We can think of the breakdown in the choreography of various spheres of life as a matter of concern, to borrow a phrase from Latour (2004), not as a matter of fact (there is no fact universal to all spheres). Having already discussed night work at length, let us recapitulate previous matters of concern discussed earlier in the book.

## Disconnections of a Connected World

In Gurgaon we saw the case of a city that has functionally differentiated to such an extent that it has turned into functional clusters of mini cities, SEZs, and malls—neat, fully functional packages of life. These differentiated domains, constructed for different purposes, seemed to have crowded out public, nonconsumption spaces. While displaying many characteristics of Marc Augé's (1995) nonplaces, Gurgaon goes beyond and extends the notion. Augé contrasts the notion of "anthropological places"—or places formed through identity and memory—with "non-places," which are proliferating throughout the globe: shopping malls, airports, airplanes, hotels, highways, and cyberspace, where we spend an ever-increasing proportion of our lives. Some emerging descriptions of Gurgaon are strikingly close: "cyber city" or "the mall capital of India." But Gurgaon stretches Augé's notion of nonplace by inserting itself in the time zones of other places. It does not merely tell what time it is in other cities, as we see in airports; some of its population exists in those time zones. Clients of call centers reside mostly in the United States, United Kingdom, and Australia, and to a much smaller degree in non-English-speaking countries (some call centers do serve in languages other than English, employing graduates of foreign-language institutes in India, typically for real-time text-based queries). The nighttime economy of call centers, to a great degree, is governed by programs of the world across the globe.

A city of many enclaves, Gurgaon, in its functional connections to other parts of the world, shows persistent disconnections within its geography. It breaks down the linearity of the modern cities where basic amenities—electricity to water—were made available to all residents irrespective of the class divide. No longer a local city where people's identity is connected to the region's history and its community, Gurgaon—aptly named a "millennium city"—appears to represent a new kind of urban formation in the emerging world society.

Gurgaon's call centers have developed a global mode of communication conducted in what they term a neutral accent, a functional move to connect previously unconnected parts of the world. Yet, in this very integration, they appear to be engaged in processes that disintegrate previous clusters of languages, accents, norms, and values, replacing them with economically oriented communication. Ninety percent of the world's languages are expected to disappear in the twenty-first century (Nettle and Romaine 2000). In chapter 3 on neutral accent I sought to resolve the question of what made cross-continental communication possible by examining two processes, neutralization and mimesis, in conjunction with each other. In order to realize their global potential, call centers seek to find a common ground for communication. If no such ground exists, it is produced by neutralizing the sociocultural particularity of personhood and substantiating through mimesis the functionally oriented systemic communication with everyday sociality. India's call centers employ a dual strategy of neutralizing unwanted cultural elements from communication while also training agents in foreign cultures whose basic frameworks often remain inaccessible to agents. The complexity of culture created the pressure to make selections, and mimesis was a particular form of cultural selections that call centers needed in order to facilitate real-time communication across continents. As opposed to everyday conversations within culturally shared frames, Gurgaon's call centers may help us understand certain emergent processes of global communication, and may hint at how the world will talk in the future.

Just as imperatives of global communication require a trained change in the agents' language and accent, their overseas customers, too, must be transformed for the purpose. While they are not directly trained, the development of their system identities solves the problem of connecting with the right profiles. Multiple functional enclaves of identity—financial, medical, work, or consumption—seem to proliferate, allowing global connections through software dialers. Yet system identities also seem to harbor a disconnect—including identity thefts—with social, cultural, psychological, and political differences that often undergird personhood.

While accounts of globalization are accounts of integrations, a fast globalizing world will also have its accidents, which may not look like industrial accidents with visible physical injuries but their effects will be felt in the social, psychological, and physical realms. With global integration comes a disintegration of the self from its place of socialization and meaning. Just as industrial society developed extensive regulation, insurance, and compensation schemes against its accidents, global information society will need to develop its own global institutions, practices, laws, and regulations. It will not be sufficient to focus on the digital divide, still existing in isolated parts of the world, or failures of integration. It will be of equal importance to focus on the problems associated with the success of integration, of digital connection, of global networks, and of their myriad effects.

# REFERENCES

AAP. 2011. "Babies and Toddlers Should Learn from Play, not Screens." *American Academcy of Pediatrics News Release*. Accessed on January 10, 2013. http://www2.aap.org/pressroom/mediaunder2.pdf.

Abbate, Janet. 1999. *Inventing the Internet*. Cambridge, MA: MIT Press.

Akerstedt, T., G. Kecklund, and L. G. Horte. 2001. "Night Driving, Season, and the Risk of Highway Accidents." *Sleep* 24:401–6.

Akerstedt, Torbjorn, Bjorn Peters, Anna Anund, and Goran Kecklund. 2005. "Impaired Alertness and Performance Driving Home from the Night Shift: A Driving Simulator Study." *Journal of Sleep Research* 14 (1): 17–20.

Alexander, Jeffrey C., and Paul Burbank Colomy. 1990. *Differentiation Theory and Social Change: Comparative and Historical Perspectives*. New York: Columbia University Press.

Aneesh, A. 1999. "Technologically Embedded Authority: The Post-Industrial Decline in Bureaucratic Hierarchies." Paper presented at the Annual Meeting of the *American Sociological Association*, August.

Aneesh, A. 2001. "Skill Saturation: Rationalization and Post-industrial Work." *Theory and Society* 30 (3): 363–96.

Aneesh, A. 2006. *Virtual Migration: The Programming of Globalization*. Durham, NC: Duke University Press.

Aneesh, A. 2007. "Specters of Global Communication." *Frakcija* 43/44:26–33.

Aneesh, A. 2009. "Global Labor: Algocratic Modes of Organization." *Sociological Theory* 27 (4): 347–70.

Aneesh, A. 2012. "Negotiating Globalization: Men and Women of India's Call Centers." *Journal of Social Issues* 68 (3): 514–33.

Appadurai, Arjun. 1988. "Introduction: Place and Voice in Anthropological Theory." *Cultural Anthropology* 3 (1): 16–20.

Aschoff, Jürgen. 1981. *Handbook of Behavioral Neurobiology: Biological Rhythms*, vol. 4. New York: Plenum Press.

Augé, Marc. 1995. *Non-Places: Introduction to an Anthropology of Supermodernity*. London: Verso.

Austin, J. L. 1962. *How to Do Things with Words*. Oxford: Clarendon Press.

Bachelard, Gaston. 1964. *The Poetics of Space*. New York: Orion Press.

Baker, Stephen. 2008. *The Numerati*. Boston: Houghton Mifflin.

Bankrate. 2013. "Smart Spending: February 2013 Financial Index Charts." Accessed on May 13, 2013. http://www.bankrate.com/finance/consumer-index/financial-security-charts-0213.aspx.

Barley, Stephen R. 1983. "Semiotics and the Study of Occupational and Organizational Cultures." *Administrative Science Quarterly* 28 (3): 393–413.

Bar-on, Miriam. 2000. "The Effects of Television on Child Health: Implications and Recommendations." *Archives of Disease in Childhood* 83 (4): 289.

Basi, J. K. Tina. 2009. *Women, Identity and India's Call Centre Industry*. London: Routledge.

Batt, Rosemary, Virginia Doellgast, and Hyunji Kwon. 2005. "Service Management and Employment Systems in U.S. and Indian Call Centers." *Faculty Publications—Human Resource Studies* Paper 39, Cornell University. Accessed on December 1, 2012. http://digitalcommons.ilr.cornell.edu/hrpubs/39.

Berger, Peter L., and Thomas Luckmann. 1990. *The Social Construction of Reality: A Treatise in the Sociology of Knowledge*. New York: Anchor Books.

Bhagwati, J., A. Panagariya, and T. N. Srinivasan. 2004. "The Muddles over Outsourcing." *Journal of Economic Perspectives* 18 (4): 93–114.

Birth, Kevin. 2007. "Time and the Biological Consequences of Globalization." *Current Anthropology* 48:215–36.

Boellstorff, Tom. 2008. *Coming of Age in Second Life: An Anthropologist Explores the Virtually Human*. Princeton, NJ: Princeton University Press.

Bonnefond, Anne, Patricia Tassi, Joceline Roge, and Alain Muzet. 2004. "A Critical Review of Techniques Aiming at Enhancing and Sustaining Worker's Alertness during the Night Shift." *Industrial Health* 42 (1): 1–14.

Bourdieu, Pierre. 1984. *Distinction: A Social Critique of the Judgement of Taste*. Cambridge, MA: Harvard University Press.

Bourdieu, Pierre. 1986. "The Forms of Capital." In *Handbook of Theory and Research for the Sociology of Education*, edited by J. Richardson, 241–58. New York: Greenwood.

Braverman, Harry. 1974. *Labor and Monopoly Capital: The Degradation of Work in the Twentieth Century*. New York: Monthly Review Press.

Brenner, Neil. 2004. *New State Spaces: Urban Governance and the Rescaling of Statehood*. New York: Oxford University Press.

Burgess, H. J., K. M. Sharkey, and C. I. Eastman. 2002. "Bright Light, Dark and Melatonin Can Promote Circadian Adaptation in Night Shift Workers." *Sleep Medicine Reviews* 6 (5): 407–20.

Butler, Judith. 1990. *Gender Trouble: Feminism and the Subversion of Identity*. New York: Routledge.

Carrara, Sandro, Léandre Bolomey, Cristina Boero, Andrea Cavallini, Eric Meurville, Giovanni De Micheli, Tanja Rezzonico, Michele Proietti, and Fabio Grassi. 2011. "Single-metabolite Bio-Nano-Sensors and System for Remote Monitoring in Animal Models." IEEE *Sensors*, 716–19.

Cerulo, Karen A. 1997. "Identity Construction: New Issues, New Directions." *Annual Review of Sociology* 23:385–409.

Chao, Elaine L. 2001. *Report on the American Workforce*. Washington, DC: Department of Labor.

Chesley, Noelle. 2005. "Blurring Boundaries? Linking Technology Use, Spillover, Individual Distress, and Family Satisfaction." *Journal of Marriage and Family* 67 (5): 1237–48.

Clarke, Roger. 1994. "The Digital Persona and Its Application to Data Surveillance." *Information Society* 10 (2): 77–92.

Coase, Ronald H. 1937. "The Nature of the Firm." *Economica* 4:386–405.

Cole, Simon A., and Henry Pontell. 2006. "'Don't Be Low Hanging Fruit': Identity Theft as Moral Panic." In *Surveillance and Security: Technological Politics and Power in Everyday Life*, edited by Torin Monahan, 125–47. New York: Routledge.

Cong, Peng, Nattapon Chaimanonart, Wen H. Ko, and Darrin J. Young. 2009. "A Wireless and Batteryless 10-Bit Implantable Blood Pressure Sensing Microsystem with Adaptive RF Powering for Real-Time Laboratory Mice Monitoring." IEEE *Journal of Solid-State Circuits* 44:3631–36441.

Cooley, Charles Horton. 1902. *Human Nature and the Social Order*. New York: Scribner.

Costa, Giovanni. 1997. "The Problem: Shiftwork." *Chronobiology International* 14 (2): 89–98.

Costello, Carrie Yang. 2005. *Professional Identity Crisis: Race, Class, Gender, and Success at Professional Schools*. Nashville, TN: Vanderbilt University Press.

Cowie, Claire. 2007. "The Accents of Outsourcing: The Meanings of 'Ineutralî in the Indian Call Centre Industry." *World Englishes* 26 (3): 316–30.

Curie, T., V. Mongrain, S. Dorsaz, G. M. Mang, Y. Emmenegger, and P. Franken. 2013. "Homeostatic and Circadian Contribution to EEG and Molecular State Variables of Sleep Regulation." *Sleep* 36 (3): 311–23.

Das, D., R. Dharwadkar, and P. Brandes. 2008. "'The Importance of Being Indian': Identity Centrality and Work Outcomes in an Off-shored Call Center in India." *Human Relations* 61 (11): 1499.

Davis, Scott, Dana K. Mirick, Chu Chen, and Frank Z. Stanczyk. 2012. "Night Shift Work and Hormone Levels in Women." *Cancer Epidemiology Biomarkers and Prevention* 21 (4): 609–18.

de Certeau, Michel. 1984. *The Practice of Everyday Life.* Berkeley: University of California Press.

Deibert, Ronald J. 2013. *Black Code: Inside the Battle for Cyberspace.* New York: Random House.

Deleuze, Gilles. 1994. *Difference and Repetition.* New York: Columbia University Press.

Deleuze, Gilles, and Félix Guattari. 1987. *A Thousand Plateaus.* Minneapolis: University of Minnesota Press.

Dhankhar, Leena. 2012. "Identity Theft Cases on the Rise." *Hindustan Times,* September 18.

DiMaggio, Paul, and Walter W. Powell. 1983. "The Iron Cage Revisited: Collective Rationality and Institutional Isomorphism in Organizational Fields." *American Sociological Review* 48 (2): 147–60.

DLF. 2012. "DLF Gardencity." Accessed October 29, 2012. http://www.dlfgardencity .com/landing/index.html.

DLF. 2013. "DLF Building India." Accessed November 27, 2013. http://dlf.in/dlf/ wcm/connect/Sez/sezs/sezs.

Dreyfus, H. L., S. E. Dreyfus, and T. Athanasiou. 2000. *Mind over Machine: The Power of Human Intuition and Expertise in the Era of the Computer.* New York: Simon and Schuster.

Dreyfus, Hubert L. 1979. *What Computers Can't Do: The Limits of Artificial Intelligence.* New York: Harper and Row.

Drori, Gili S., John W. Meyer, and Hokyu Hwang, eds. 2006. *Globalization and Organization: World Society and Organizational Change.* Oxford: Oxford University Press.

Du Bois, W. E. B. 2003. *The Souls of Black Folk.* New York: Fine Communications.

Dugal, Chandni. 2008. "Shops and Establishments Rules Need to Be Updated, Made Uniform." *Live Mint,* April 14. Accessed on November 28, 2012. http:// www.livemint.com/Politics/9vfzDV2zmPFRacUeUHLLoO/Management—Shops -and-establishments-rules-need-to-be-updat.html.

Economist. 2012. "The Debtors' Merry-go-round." http://www.economist.com/ node/21543191.

Edwards, Richard. 1979. *Contested Terrain: The Transformation of the Workplace in the Twentieth Century.* New York: Basic Books.

eHealth. 2013. "Smoking Status and Body Mass Index Relative to Average Individual Health Insurance Premiums." *An addendum to the November 2012 eHealth report, "The Cost and Benefits of Individual and Family Health Insurance Plans."* http://news .ehealthinsurance.com/_ir/68/20125/Smoking_Status_BMI_and_Individual _Health_Insurance_Premiums.pdf.

ET. 2007. Yoga Stress Buster for BPO Cabbies! *Economic Times,* October 24.

FE. 2002. "Call Centres May Get Wake-Up Call over Shops Act." *Financial Express*, December 2.

Feld, Steven. 1996. "Waterfall of Song: An Acoustemology of Place Resounding in Bosavi, Papua New Guinea." In *Senses of Place*, edited by Steven Feld and Keith Basso. Santa Fe, NM: School of American Research Press.

Feld, Steven, and Keith H. Basso, eds. 1996. *Senses of Place*. Santa Fe, NM: School of American Research Press.

Femina. 2005. "Working the Graveyard Shift." *Femina*, Fitness Section, March 1, 56–57.

Fenno, Richard F. 1978. *Home Style: House Members in Their Districts*. Boston: Little, Brown.

Ferguson, James G. 1999. *Expectations of Modernity: Myths and Meanings of Urban Life on the Zambian Copperbelt*. Berkeley: University of California Press.

Ferguson, James G., and Akhil Gupta. 1992. "Beyond 'Culture': Space, Identity, and the Politics of Difference." *Cultural Anthropology* 7 (1): 6–23.

Finklea, Kristin M. 2012. "Identity Theft: Trends and Issues: Congressional Research Service Report for Congress." *Statistics and Computing* 14 (3): 15.

Foner, Philip S. 1986. *May Day: A Short History of the International Worker's Holiday, 1886–1986*. New York: International Publishers.

Foucault, Michel. 1979. *Discipline and Punish*. New York: Vintage Books.

Franken, P., and D.-J. Dijk. 2009. "Circadian Clock Genes and Sleep Homeostasis." *European Journal of Neuroscience* 29 (9): 1820–29.

Freeman, Carla. 2000. *High Tech and High Heels in the Global Economy: Women, Work, and Pink-Collar Identities in the Caribbean*. Durham, NC: Duke University Press.

Froehle, Craig M. 2006. "Service Personnel, Technology, and Their Interaction in Influencing Customer Satisfaction." *Decision Sciences* 37 (1): 5.

Fujimura, Joan H. 1996. *Crafting Science: A Sociohistory of the Quest for the Genetics of Cancer*. Cambridge, MA: Harvard University Press.

Gerstner, Jason R., William M. Vanderheyden, Timothy LaVaute, Cara J. Westmark, Labib Rouhana, Allan I. Pack, Marv Wickens, and Charles F. Landry. 2012. "Time of Day Regulates Subcellular Trafficking, Tripartite Synaptic Localization, and Polyadenylation of the Astrocytic Fabp7 mRNA." *Journal of Neuroscience* 32 (4): 1383–94.

Glaeser, Andreas. 2005. "An Ontology for the Ethnographic Analysis of Social Processes." *Social Analysis* 49 (3): 16–45.

Goffman, Erving. 1959. *The Presentation of Self in Everyday Life*. Garden City, NY: Doubleday.

Goffman, Erving. 1967. *Interaction Ritual: Essays in Face-to-Face Behavior*. Chicago: Aldine.

GOI. 2005. "The Special Economic Zones Act, 2005," 28.

Gold, D. R., S. Rogacz, N. Bock, T. D. Tosteson, T. M. Baum, F. E. Speizer, and C. A. Czeisler. 1992. "Rotating Shift Work, Sleep, and Accidents Related to Sleepiness in Hospital Nurses." *American Journal of Public Health* 82:1011–14.

Gonigal, George. 2010. "SEZ Boom in Gurgaon." *EZine Articles*. Accessed March 1, 2011. http://ezinearticles.com/about.html.

Granovetter, Mark. 1985. "Economic Action and Social Structure: The Problem of Embeddedness." *American Journal of Sociology* 91 (3): 481–510.

Hacking, Ian. 1999. *The Social Construction of What?* Cambridge, MA: Harvard University Press.

Haggerty, Kevin, and Richard Ericson. 2000. "The Surveillant Assemblage." *British Journal of Sociology* 51 (4): 605–22.

Hansen, Johnni. 2001. "Increased Breast Cancer Risk among Women Who Work Predominantly at Night." *Epidemiology* 12 (1): 74–77.

Haraway, Donna Jeanne. 1991. *Simians, Cyborgs, and Women: The Reinvention of Nature.* New York: Routledge.

Haraway, Donna Jeanne. 1991. "A Cyborg Manifesto: Science, Technology and Socialist-Feminism in the Late Twentieth Century." In *Simians, Cyborgs, and Women*, 149–82. New York: Routledge.

Haraway, Donna Jeanne. 1997. *Modest_witness@second_millennium.femaleman_meets _oncomouse: Feminism and Technoscience.* New York: Routledge.

Harding, Sandra. 1992. "After the Neutrality Ideal: Science, Politics, and 'Strong Objectivity.'" *Social Research* 59 (3): 567–87.

Hardt, Michael. 1999. "Affective Labor." *Boundary 2* 26 (2): 89–100.

Harvard. 2013. "Waking up to Sleep's Role in Weight Control." Accessed on April 5, 2013. http://www.hsph.harvard.edu/obesity-prevention-source/obesity-causes/sleep-and-obesity/.

Harvey, David. [1982]. 2007. *The Limits to Capital.* New York: Verso.

Hegel, Georg Wilhelm Friedrich. 2001. *Philosophy of Right.* Kitchener, Ontario: Batoche Books.

Hillman, C. H., K. I. Erickson, and A. F. Kramer. 2008. "Be Smart, Exercise Your Heart: Exercise Effects on Brain and Cognition." *Nature Reviews Neuroscience* 9 (1): 58–65.

Hochschild, Arlie Russell. 1983. *The Managed Heart: Commercialization of Human Feeling.* Berkeley: University of California Press.

Horne, J. A., and L. A. Reyner. 1995. "Sleep Related Vehicle Accidents." *British Medical Journal* 310:565–67.

Huttenlocher, Peter R. 2002. *Neural Plasticity: The Effects of Environment on the Development of the Cerebral Cortex.* Cambridge, MA: Harvard University Press.

I. D. Analytics. 2012. "Identities of Nearly 2.5 Million Deceased Americans Misused Each Year." http://www.idanalytics.com/news-and-events/news-releases/2012/4-23-2012.php.

Jain, Sarah Lochlann. 2006. *Injury: The Politics of Product Design and Safety Law in the United States.* Princeton, NJ: Princeton University Press.

Knorr Cetina, Karin, and U. Bruegger. 2002. "Global Microstructures: The Virtual Societies of Financial Markets." *American Journal of Sociology* 107 (4): 905–50.

Krishnamurthy, M. 2004. "Resources and Rebels: A Study of Identity Management in Indian Call Centers." *Anthropology of Work Review* 25 (3–4): 9–18.

Krücken, George, and G. S. Drori. 2009. *World Society: The Writings of John W. Meyer*. New York: Oxford University Press.

Kubo, Tatsuhiko, Kotaro Ozasa, Kazuya Mikami, Kenji Wakai, Yoshihisa Fujino, Yoshiyuki Watanabe, Tsuneharu Miki, Masahiro Nakao, Kyohei Hayashi, and Koji Suzuki. 2006. "Prospective Cohort Study of the Risk of Prostate Cancer among Rotating-Shift Workers: Findings from the Japan Collaborative Cohort Study." *American Journal of Epidemiology* 164 (6): 549–55.

Lakoff, George, and Mark Johnson. 1999. *Philosophy in the Flesh: The Embodied Mind and Its Challenge to Western Thought*. New York: Basic Books.

Lakoff, George, and Rafael E. Núñez. 2000. *Where Mathematics Comes From: How the Embodied Mind Brings Mathematics into Being*. New York: Basic Books.

Lancry, Alain, and Marie-Hélène Stoklosa. 1995. "Les effets d'une pause sur la vigilance et l'efficience au travail." *Le Travail Humain* 58: 71–83.

Langston, Richard. 2013. "Palimpsests of Sixty-Eight: Theorizing Labor after Adorno." In *The Long 1968: Revisions and New Perspectives*, edited by Daniel J. Sherman, Ruud van Dijk, Jamine Alinder, and A. Aneesh. Bloomington: Indiana University Press.

Latour, Bruno. 1993. *We Have Never Been Modern*. Cambridge, MA: Harvard University Press.

Latour, Bruno. 1994. "On Technical Mediation—Philosophy, Sociology, Genealogy." *Common Knowledge* 3:29–64.

Latour, Bruno. 2004. "Why Has Critique Run Out of Steam? From Matters of Fact to Matters of Concern." *Critical Inquiry* 30 (2): 225–48.

Lechner, Frank J., and John Boli. 2005. *World Culture: Origins and Consequences*. Malden, MA: Blackwell.

Lee, Susie, Lawrence A. Donehower, Alan J. Herron, David D. Moore, and Loning Fu. 2010. "Disrupting Circadian Homeostasis of Sympathetic Signaling Promotes Tumor Development in Mice." *PLoS ONE* 5 (6): e10995.

Leidner, Robin. 1993. *Fast Food, Fast Talk: Service Work and the Routinization of Everyday Life*. Berkeley: University of California Press.

Lessig, Lawrence. 1999. *Code and Other Laws of Cyberspace*. New York: Basic Books.

Lille, F., and P. Andlauer. 1981. "Rythmes circadiens, sommeil veille et travail." In *Précis de physiologie du travail, Notions d'ergonomie*, edited by J. Scherrer, 485–504. Paris: Elsevier Masson.

Lohr, Steve, and John Markoff. 2010. "Computers Learn to Listen, and Some Talk Back." *New York Times*, June 24.

Luhmann, Niklas. 1984. *Social Systems*. Palo Alto, CA: Stanford University Press.

Lyon, David. 1994. *The Electronic Eye: The Rise of Surveillance Society*. Minneapolis: University of Minnesota Press.

Lyon, David, ed. 2002. *Surveillance as Social Sorting*. New York: Routledge.

Macaulay, Thomas Babington. 1967. "Indian Education: Minute of the 2nd of February, 1835." In *Macaulay: Prose and Poetry*, edited by G. M. Young. Cambridge, MA: Harvard University Press.

Marian, V., M. Spivey, and J. Hirsch. 2003. "Shared and Separate Systems in Bilingual Language Processing: Converging Evidence from Eyetracking and Brain Imaging." *Brain and Language* 86 (1): 70–82.

Martin, John Levi. 2003. "What Is Field Theory? 1." *American Journal of Sociology* 109 (1): 1–49.

Martin, John Levi. 2011. *The Explanation of Social Action*. Oxford: Oxford University Press.

Marx, Gary. 1989. *Undercover: Police Surveillance in America*. Berkeley: University of California Press.

Marx, Karl. 1967. "Economic and Philosophic Manuscript of 1844." *Writings of the Young Marx on Philosophy and Society*, edited by Loyd David Easton and Kurt H. Guddat, ix, 506. Garden City, NY: Doubleday.

Marx, Karl. 2004. *Capital: A Critique of Political Economy, Vol. I*. London: Penguin.

McLuhan, Marshall. [1964]. 1994. *Understanding Media: The Extensions of Man*. Cambridge, MA: MIT Press.

Mead, George Herbert. 1913. "The Social Self." *Journal of Philosophy, Psychology, and Scientific Methods* 10:374–80.

Mead, George Herbert. 1922. "A Behavioristic Account of the Significant Symbol." *Journal of Philosophy* 19 (6): 157–63.

Mead, George Herbert. 1934. *Mind, Self and Society from the Standpoint of a Social Behaviorist*. Chicago: University of Chicago Press.

Megdal, Sarah P., Candyce H. Kroenke, Francine Laden, Eero Pukkala, and Eva S. Schernhammer. 2005. "Night Work and Breast Cancer Risk: A Systematic Review and Meta-Analysis." *European Journal of Cancer* 41 (13): 2023–32.

Melbin, Murray. 1987. *Night as Frontier: Colonizing the World after Dark*. New York: Free Press.

Merton, Robert King. 1968. *Social Theory and Social Structure*. New York: Free Press.

Meyer, John W. 2009. "Reflections: Institutional Theory and World Society." In *World Society: The Writings of John W. Meyer*, edited by Georg Krücken and Gili S. Drori, 36–63.

Meyer, John W., John Boli, George M. Thomas, and F. O. Ramirez. 1997. "World Society and the Nation-State." *American Journal of Sociology* 103 (1): 144–81.

Meyer, John W., and Brian Rowan. 1977. "Institutionalized Organizations: Formal Structure as Myth and Ceremony." *American Journal of Sociology* 83 (2): 340–63.

Mirchandani, K. 2005. "Gender Eclipsed? Racial Hierarchies in Transnational Call Center Work." *Social Justice* 32 (4): 105.

Mirchandani, Kiran. 2012. *Phone Clones: Authenticity Work in the Transnational Service Economy*. Ithaca, NY: Cornell University Press.

Mitra, Sankar. 2011. "Does Evening Sun Increase the Risk of Skin Cancer?" *Proceedings of the National Academy of Sciences* 108 (47): 18857–58.

Miyauchi, F., K. Nanjo, and K. Otsuka. 1992. "Effects of Night Shift on Plasma Concentrations of Melatonin, LH, FSH and Prolactin, and Menstrual Irregularity." *Japanese Journal of Industrial Health* 34:545–50.

Mukherjee, Sanjukta. 2008. "Producing the Knowledge Professional: Gendered Geographies of Alienation in India's New High-Tech Workplace." In *In an Outpost of the Global Economy: Work and Workers in India's Information Technology Industry*, edited by Carol Upadhya and A. R. Vasavi. New Delhi: Routledge India.

Nadeem, Shehzad. 2011. *Dead Ringers: How Outsourcing Is Changing the Way Indians Understand Themselves*. Princeton, NJ: Princeton University Press.

Nakamura, Lisa. 2008. *Digitizing Race: Visual Cultures of the Internet*. Minneapolis: University of Minnesota Press.

Nass, Clifford Ivar, and Scott Brave. 2005. *Wired for Speech: How Voice Activates and Advances the Human-Computer Relationship*. Cambridge, MA: MIT Press.

Nasscom. 2000. *Indian Directory of IT-Enabled Service Providers*. New Delhi: Nasscom.

Nasscom. 2011. "The IT BPO Sector in India: Strategic Review." New Delhi: Nasscom.

Negroponte, Nicholas. 1995. *Being Digital*. New York: Knopf.

Nettle, Daniel, and Suzanne Romaine. 2000. *Vanishing Voices: The Extinction of the World's Languages*. New York: Oxford University Press.

Newton, Isaac. 2004. *Isaac Newton: Philosophical Writings*, edited by Andrew Janiak. Cambridge: Cambridge University Press.

Noronha, Ernesto, and Premilla D'Cruz. 2007. "Reconciling Dichotomous Demands: Telemarketing Agents in Bangalore and Mumbai, India." *Qualitative Report* 12 (2): 255–80.

Nurminen, Tuula. 1998. "Shift Work and Reproductive Health." *Scandinavian Journal of Work, Environment and Health* 24 (3): 28–34.

Ohayon, M. M., P. Lemoine, V. Arnaud-Briant, and M. Dreyfus. 2002. "Prevalence and Consequences of Sleep Disorders in a Shift Worker Population." *Journal of Psychosomatic Research* 53:577–83.

Palit, A., and S. Bhattacharjee. 2008. *Special Economic Zones in India: Myths and Realities*. New Delhi: Anthem Press India.

Parsons, Talcott. 1968. "Social Interaction." *International Encyclopedia of the Social Sciences* 7:429–41.

Parsons, Talcott, and Edward Shils. 1951. *Toward a General Theory of Action*. Cambridge, MA: Harvard University Press.

Patel, Reena. 2010. *Working the Night Shift: Women in India's Call Center Industry*. Palo Alto, CA: Stanford University Press.

Patel, Sanjay R., Atul Malhotra, David P. White, Daniel J. Gottlieb, and Frank B. Hu. 2006. "Association between Reduced Sleep and Weight Gain in Women." *American Journal of Epidemiology* 164 (10): 947–54.

Pellegrini, A. D., and P. K. Smith. 1998. "Physical Activity Play: The Nature and Function of a Neglected Aspect of Play." *Child Development* 69 (3): 577–98.

Pettigrew, A. M. 1979. "On Studying Organizational Cultures." *Administrative Science Quarterly* 24 (4): 570–81.

Pick, D., and D. Müller. 2011. "Retailing in India: Background, Challenges, Prospects." *European Retail Research* 25 (1): 107.

Pinch, Trevor J., and Frank Trocco. 2004. *Analog Days: The Invention and Impact of the Moog Synthesizer.* Cambridge, MA: Harvard University Press.

Pollan, Michael. 2007. "Unhappy Meals." *New York Times*, January 28.

Poster, Winifred. 2007. "Who's on the Line? Indian Call Center Agents Pose as Americans for US-Outsourced Firms." *Industrial Relations: A Journal of Economy and Society* 46 (2): 271–304.

Poster, W. R., and G. Wilson. 2008. "Introduction: Race, Class, and Gender in Transnational Labor Inequality." *American Behavioral Scientist* 52 (3): 295.

Powell, Walter W. 1990. "Neither Market nor Hierarchy: Network Forms of Organization." *Research in Organizational Behaviour* 12:295–336.

Presser, Harriet B. 2003. *Working in a 24/7 Economy: Challenges for American Families.* New York: Russell Sage Foundation.

Prügl, Elisabeth. 1999. *The Global Construction of Gender: Home-Based Work in the Political Economy of the 20th Century.* New York: Columbia University Press.

Putnam, Hilary. 1995. *Pragmatism: An Open Question.* Oxford: Blackwell.

Richardson, G. S., J. D. Miner, and C. A. Czeisler. 1990. "Impaired Driving Performance in Shiftworkers: The Role of the Circadian System in a Multifactorial Model." *Alcohol Drugs Driving* 5 (4): 265–73.

Rivas, Cecilia Maribel. 2007. "Imaginaries of Transnationalism: Media and Cultures of Consumption in El Salvador." Ph.D. diss., University of California, San Diego.

Rivero, Yeidy. 2011. "Mediating 'Neutrality': Latino Diasporic Films." In *Beyond Globalization: Making New Worlds in Media, Art, and Social Practices*, edited by A. Aneesh, Lane Hall, and Patrice Petro, 103–20. New Brunswick, NJ: Rutgers University Press.

Sassen, Saskia. 1991. *The Global City: New York, London, Tokyo.* Princeton, NJ: Princeton University Press.

Sassen, Saskia. 2007. *A Sociology of Globalization.* New York: W. W. Norton.

Schernhammer, Eva S., Francine Laden, Frank E. Speizer, Walter C. Willett, David J. Hunter, Ichiro Kawachi, and Graham A. Colditz. 2001. "Rotating Night Shifts and Risk of Breast Cancer in Women Participating in the Nurses' Health Study." *Journal of the National Cancer Institute* 93 (20): 1563–68.

Schernhammer, Eva S., Francine Laden, Frank E. Speizer, Walter C. Willett, David J. Hunter, Ichiro Kawachi, Charles S. Fuchs, and Graham A. Colditz. 2003. "Night-shift Work and Risk of Colorectal Cancer in the Nurses' Health Study." *Journal of the National Cancer Institute* 95 (11): 825–28.

Schutz, Alfred. 1973. *The Structures of the Life-World*. Evanston, IL: Northwestern University Press.

Scott, Allene J., and J. LaDou. 1989. "Shiftwork: Effects on Sleep and Health with Recommendations for Medical Surveillance and Screening." *Occupational Medicine* 5 (2): 273–99.

Scott, James C. 1998. *Seeing Like a State: How Certain Schemes to Improve the Human Condition Have Failed*. New Haven, CT: Yale University Press.

Searle, John R. 1995. *The Construction of Social Reality*. New York: Free Press.

Selznick, Philip, ed. 1980. *TVA and the Grass Roots: A Study of Politics and Organization*. Berkeley: University of California Press.

Sennet, Richard. 1970. *The Uses of Disorder*. New York: Alfred A. Knopf.

Shephard, R. J., H. LaVallee, M. Volle, R. LaBarre, and C. Beaucage. 1994. "Academic Skills and Required Physical Education: The Trois Rivieres Experience." *CAHPER Research Supplement* 1 (1): 1–12.

Shubin, Neil. 2013. *The Universe Within: A Scientific Adventure*. New York: Pantheon Books.

Simmel, Georg. 1903. "The Metropolis and Mental Life." In *The Blackwell City Reader*, edited by Gary Bridge and Sophie Watson. Malden, MA: Wiley-Blackwell.

Simon, Bar. 2005. "The Return of Panopticism: Supervision, Subjection and the New Surveillance." *Surveillance and Society* 3 (1): 1–20.

Singer, Natasha. 2012. "Your Attention, Bought in an Instant." *New York Times*, November 18, BU1.

Slater, Don, and Fran Tonkiss. 2001. *Market Society: Markets and Modern Social Theory*. Cambridge: Polity.

Smircich, L. 1983. "Concepts of Culture and Organizational Analysis." *Administrative Science Quarterly* 28 (3): 339–58.

Smith, Dorothy E. 1987. *The Everyday World as Problematic: A Feminist Sociology*. Boston: Northeastern University Press.

Smith, L., S. Folkard, and C. J. M. Poole. 1994. "Increased Injuries on Night Shift." *Lancet* 344 (8930): 1137–39.

Soghoian, Chris, and Naomi Gilens. 2013. "New Document Sheds Light on Government's Ability to Search iPhones." *ACLU Free Future Blog*. Accessed on February 28, 2013. http://www.aclu.org/blog/technology-and-liberty-criminal -law-reform-immigrants-rights/new-document-sheds-light.

Srivastava, R. K. 2008. "Changing Retail Scene in India." *International Journal of Retail and Distribution Management* 36 (9): 714–21.

Stark, David. 2009. *The Sense of Dissonance: Accounts of Worth in Economic Life*. Princeton, NJ: Princeton University Press.

Stevens, Richard G. 2012. "Does Electric Light Stimulate Cancer Development in Children?" *Cancer Epidemiology Biomarkers and Prevention* 21 (5): 701–4.

Straif, Kurt, Robert Baan, Yann Grosse, Béatrice Secretan, Fatiha El Ghissassi, Véronique Bouvard, Andrea Altieri, Lamia Benbrahim-Tallaa, and Vincent

Cogliano. 2007. "Carcinogenicity of Shift-work, Painting, and Fire-fighting." *Lancet Oncology* 8 (12): 1065–66.

Stutts, J. C., J. W. Wilkins, J. Scott Osberg, and B. V. Vaughn. 2003. "Driver Risk Factors for Sleep-related Crashes." *Accident Analysis and Prevention* 35:321–31.

Suncity. 2012. "Suncity Gurgaon." Accessed on July 16, 2012. http://www .suncityprojectsltd.com/gurgaon.htm.

Tan, D. X., L. D. Chen, B. Poeggeler, L. C. Manchester, and R. J. Reiter. 1993. "Melatonin: A Potent, Endogenous Hydroxyl Radical Scavenger." *Endocrine Journal* 1 (1): 57–60.

Tan, L. H., J. A. Spinks, C. M. Feng, W. T. Siok, C. A. Perfetti, J. Xiong, P. T. Fox, and J. H. Gao. 2003. "Neural Systems of Second Language Reading Are Shaped by Native Language." *Human Brain Mapping* 18 (3): 158–66.

Taylor, P. J. 1995. "World Cities and Territorial States: The Rise and Fall of their Mutuality." *World Cities in a World System*, edited by Paul L. Knox and Peter J. Taylor, 48–62. Cambridge: Cambridge University Press.

Taylor, Phil, and Peter Bain. 2005. "'India Calling to the Far Away Towns': The Call Centre Labour Process and Globalization." *Work, Employment and Society* 19 (2): 261.

Testart, J., R. Frydman, and M. Roger. 1982. "Seasonal Influence of Diurnal Rhythms in the Onset of the Plasma Luteinizing Hormone Surge in Women." *Journal of Clinical Endocrinology and Metabolism* 55:374–77.

Thomas, J. 1984. "Cross-Cultural Discourse as 'Unequal Encounter': Towards a Pragmatic Analysis." *Applied Linguistics* 5 (3): 226–35.

TOI. 2010. "Number of Malls in India to Touch 280 in 2011–12: CBRE." Accessed on December 19, 2010. http://articles.timesofindia.indiatimes.com/2010–12–19/ india-business/28252868_1_retail-space-sq-ft-retail-rentals.

Torpey, John C. 1999. *The Invention of the Passport: Surveillance, Citizenship, and the State.* Cambridge: Cambridge University Press.

Trachtenberg, Alexander, and William Weinstone. 1931. *The History of May Day.* International pamphlets. Accessed on January 2, 2013. http://marxists.org/ subject/mayday/articles/tracht.html.

Turek, Fred W., and Phyllis C. Zee, eds. 1999. *Regulation of Sleep and Circadian Rhythms.* New York: Marcel Dekker.

Turkle, Sherry. 1995. *Life on the Screen.* New York: Simon and Schuster.

Turkle, Sherry. 2012. *Alone Together: Why We Expect More from Technology and Less from Each Other.* New York: Basic Books.

Turner, Fred. 2006. *From Counterculture to Cyberculture: Stewart Brand, the Whole Earth Network, and the Rise of Digital Utopianism.* Chicago: University of Chicago Press.

Upadhya, Carol, and A. R. Vasavi. 2008. *In an Outpost of the Global Economy: Work and Workers in India's Information Technology Industry.* New Delhi: Routledge.

Vaidya, Abhay. 2005. "India's First BPO Scam Unraveled." *Times of India*, April 23.

Valgimigli, F., F. Lucarelli, C. Scuffi, S. Morandi, and I. Sposato. 2010. "Evaluating the Clinical Accuracy of GlucoMen® Day: A Novel Microdialysis-based Continuous Glucose Monitor." *Journal of Diabetes Science and Technology* 4:1182–92.

Vishnoi, Anubhuti. 2006. "Cops Set for Night Vigil on BPO Cars Zooming the City." *Indian Express*, April 8.

Viswanathan, Akila N., Susan E. Hankinson, and Eva S. Schernhammer. 2007. "Night Shift Work and the Risk of Endometrial Cancer." *Cancer Research* 67 (21): 10618–22.

Ware, Roger, and Robert A. Baker. 1977. "The Effects of Mental Set and States of Consciousness on Vigilance Decrement: A Systematic Exploration." In *Vigilance: Theory, Operational Performance, and Physiological Correlates*, edited by Robert R. Mackie, 603–16. New York: Plenum Press.

Weber, Max. 1921. *Economy and Society: An Outline of Interpretive Sociology*. Berkeley: University of California Press.

Wellman, Barry. 1999. *Networks in the Global Village: Life in Contemporary Communities*. Boulder, CO: Westview Press.

Whaples, Robert. 1990. "Winning the Eight-Hour Day, 1909–1919." *Journal of Economic History* 50 (2): 393–406.

Williamson, Oliver. 1981. "Modern Corporations: Origins, Evolution, Attribute." *Journal of Economic Literature* 19:1539–44.

Wittgenstein, Ludwig. 1953. *Philosophical Investigations*. New York: Macmillan.

Xiang, Biao. 2007. *Global "Body Shopping": An Indian Labor System in the Information Technology Industry*. Princeton, NJ: Princeton University Press.

Zhu, Jin Liang, Niels Henrik Andersen Hjollund, Anne-Marie Nybo, and Jørn Olsen. 2004. "Shift Work, Job Stress, and Late Fetal Loss: The National Birth Cohort in Denmark." *Journal of Occupational and Environmental Medicine* 46 (11): 1144–49.

Zola, Émile. 1942. *Germinal*. London: Nonesuch Press.

Zou, Lijuan, Jubin Abutalebi, Benjamin Zinszer, Xin Yan, Hua Shu, Danling Peng, and Guosheng Ding. 2012. "Second Language Experience Modulates Functional Brain Network for the Native Language Production in Bimodal Bilinguals." *NeuroImage* 62 (3): 1367–75.